Afghanistan
1. The First Afghan War
1839–42

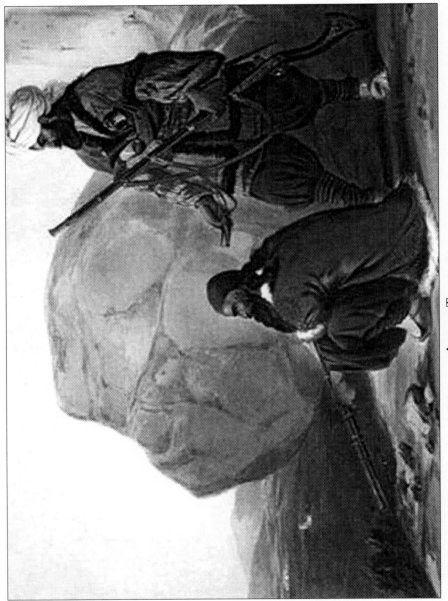

AFGHAN TRIBESMEN

Britain in Afghanistan

1. The First Afghan War
1839–42

Archibald Forbes

LEONAUR

Britain in Afghanistan 1: the First Afghan War 1839-42
by Archibald Forbes

Published by Leonaur Ltd

ISBN: 978-1-84677-304-4 (hardcover)
ISBN: 978-1-84677-303-7 (softcover)

http://www.leonaur.com

Publisher's Notes

In the interests of authenticity, the spellings, grammar and place names used have been retained from the original editions.

The opinions of the authors represent a view of events in which he was a participant related from his own perspective, as such the text is relevant as an historical document.

The views expressed in this book are not necessarily those of the publisher.

Contents

CHAPTER 1

Preliminary

Since it was the British complications with Persia which mainly furnished what pretext there was for the invasion of Afghanistan by an Anglo-Indian army in 1839, some brief recital is necessary of the relations between Great Britain and Persia prior to that aggression.

By a treaty, concluded between England and Persia in 1814, the former state bound itself, in case of the invasion of Persia by any European nation, to aid the Shah either with troops from India or by the payment of an annual subsidy in support of his war expenses. It was a dangerous engagement, even with the caveat rendering the undertaking inoperative if such invasion should be provoked by Persia. During the fierce struggle of 1825-7, between Abbas Meerza and the Russian General Paskevitch, England refrained from supporting Persia either with men or with money, and when prostrate Persia was in financial extremities because of the war indemnity which the treaty of Turkmanchai imposed upon her, England took advantage of her needs by purchasing the cancellation of the inconvenient obligation at the cheap cost of about £300,000. It was the natural result of this transaction that English influence with the Persian Court should sensibly decline, and it was not less natural that in conscious weakness Persia should fall under the domination of Russian influence.

Futteh Ali, the old Shah of Persia, died in 1834, and was succeeded by his grandson Prince Mahomed Meerza, a young man who inherited much of the ambition of his gallant father Abbas Meerza. His especial aspiration, industriously stimulated by his Russian advisers, urged him to the enterprise of conquering the independent principality of Herat, on the western border of Afghanistan. Herat was the only remnant of Afghan territory that still remained to a member of the legitimate royal house. Its ruler was Shah Kamran, son of that Mahmoud Shah who, after ousting his brother Shah Soojah from the throne of Cabul, had himself been driven from that elevation, and had retired to the minor principality of Herat. The young Shah of Persia was not destitute of justification for his designs on Herat. That this was so was frankly admitted by Mr Ellis, the British envoy to his Court, who wrote to his Government that the Shah had fair claim to the sovereignty of Afghanistan as far as Ghuznee, and that Kamran's conduct in occupying part of the Persian province of Seistan had given the Shah 'a full justification for commencing hostilities against Herat.'

The serious phase of the situation for England and India was that Russian influence was behind Persia in this hostile action against Herat. Mr Ellis pointed out that in the then existing state of relations between Persia and Russia, the progress of the former in Afghanistan was tantamount to the advancement of the latter. But unfortunately there remained valid an article in the treaty of 1814 to the effect that, in case of war between the Afghans and the Persians, the English Government should not interfere with either party unless when called on by both to mediate. In vain did Ellis and his successor M'Neill remonstrate with the Persian monarch against the Herat expedition. An appeal to St Petersburg, on the part of Great Britain, produced merely an evasive reply. How diplomatic disquietude had become intensified may be inferred from this, that whereas in April 1836 Ellis wrote of Persia as a Russian first parallel of attack against India, Lord Auckland, then Governor-General of India, directed M'Neill, in the early part of 1837, to urge the Shah to abandon his enterprise, on the ground that he (the Governor-General) 'must view with umbrage and displeasure schemes of interference and conquest on our western frontier.'

The Shah, unmoved by the representations of the British envoy, marched on Herat, and the siege was opened on November 23d, 1837. Durand, a capable critic, declares that the strength of the place, the resolution of the besiegers, the skill of their Russian military advisers, and the gallantry of the besieged, were alike objects of much exaggeration. 'The siege was from first to last thoroughly ill-conducted, and the defence, in reality not better managed, owed its *éclat* to Persian ignorance, timidity and supineness. The advice of Pottinger, the gallant English officer who assisted the defence, was seldom asked, and still more seldom taken; and no one spoke more plainly of the conduct of both besieged and besiegers than did Pottinger himself.' M'Neill effected nothing definite during a long stay in the Persian camp before Herat, the counteracting influence of the Russian envoy being too strong with the Shah; and the British representative, weary of continual slights, at length quitted the Persian camp completely foiled. After six days' bombardment, the Persians and their Russian auxiliaries delivered an assault in force on June 23d, 1838. It failed, with heavy loss, and the dispirited Shah determined on raising the siege. His resolution was quickened by the arrival of Colonel Stoddart in his camp, with the information that a military force from Bombay, supported by ships of war, had landed on the island of Karrack in the Persian Gulf, and with the peremptory ultimatum to the Shah that he must retire from Herat at once. Lord Palmerston, in ordering this diversion in the Gulf, had thought himself justified by circumstances in overriding the clear and precise terms of an article in a treaty to which England had on several occasions engaged to adhere. As for the Shah, he appears to have been relieved by the ultimatum. On the 9th September he mounted his horse and rode away from Herat. The siege had lasted nine and a half months. To-day, half a century after Simonich the Russian envoy followed Mahomed Shah from battered but unconquered Herat, that city is still an Afghan place of arms.

Shah Soojah-ool Moolk, a grandson of the illustrious Ahmed Shah, reigned in Afghanistan from 1803 till 1809. His youth had been full of trouble and vicissitude. He had been a wanderer, on the verge of starvation, a pedlar and a bandit, who raised money by plundering caravans. His courage was lightly reputed, and it was as a mere creature of circumstance that he reached the throne. His reign was perturbed, and in 1809 he was a fugitive and an exile. Runjeet Singh, the Sikh ruler of the Punjaub, defrauded him of the famous Koh-i-noor, which is now the most precious of the crown jewels of England, and plundered and imprisoned the fallen man. Shah Soojah at length escaped from Lahore. After further misfortunes he at length reached the British frontier station of Loodianah, and in 1816 became a pensioner of the East India Company.

After the downfall of Shah Soojah, Afghanistan for many years was a prey to anarchy. At length in 1826, Dost Mahomed succeeded in making himself supreme at Cabul, and this masterful man thenceforward held sway until his death in 1863, uninterruptedly save during the three years of the British occupation. Dost Mahomed was neither kith nor kin to the legitimate dynasty which he displaced. His father Poyndah Khan was an able statesman and gallant soldier. He left twenty-one sons, of whom Futteh Khan was the eldest, and Dost Mahomed one of the youngest. Futteh Khan was the Warwick of Afghanistan, but the Afghan 'Kingmaker' had no Barnet as the closing scene of his chequered life. Falling into hostile hands, he was blinded and scalped. Refusing to betray his brothers, he was leisurely cut to pieces by the order and in the presence of the monarch whom he had made. His young brother Dost Mahomed undertook to avenge his death. After years of varied fortunes the Dost had worsted all his enemies, and in 1826 he became the ruler of Cabul. Throughout his long reign Dost Mahomed was a strong and wise ruler. His youth had been neglected and dissolute. His education was defective, and he had been addicted to wine. Once seated on the throne, the reformation of our Henry Fifth was not more thorough than was that of Dost Mahomed. He taught himself to read and write, studied the Koran, became scrupulously abstemious, assiduous in affairs, no longer truculent but courteous. He is said to have made a public acknowledgment of the errors of his previous life, and a firm profession of reformation; nor did his after life belie the pledges to which he committed himself. There was a fine rugged honesty in his nature, and a streak of genuine chivalry; notwithstanding the despite he suffered at our hands, he had a real regard for the English, and his loyalty to us was broken only by his armed support of the Sikhs in the second Punjaub war.

The fallen Shah Soojah, from his asylum in Loodianah, was continually intriguing for his restoration. His schemes were long inoperative, and it was not until 1832 that certain arrangements were entered into between him and the Maharaja Runjeet Singh. To an application on Shah Soojah's part for countenance and pecuniary aid, the Anglo-Indian Government replied that to afford him assistance would be inconsistent with the policy of neutrality which the Government had imposed on itself; but it unwisely contributed financially toward his undertaking by granting him four months' pension in advance. Sixteen thousand rupees formed a scant war fund with which to attempt the recovery of a throne, but the Shah started on his errand in February 1833. After a successful contest with the Ameers of Scinde, he marched on Candahar, and besieged that fortress. Candahar was in extremity when Dost Mahomed, hurrying from Cabul, relieved it, and joining forces with its defenders, he defeated and routed Shah Soojah, who fled precipitately, leaving behind him his artillery and camp equipage, During the Dost's absence in the south, Runjeet Singh's troops crossed the Attock, occupied the Afghan province of Peshawur, and drove the Afghans into the Khyber Pass. No subsequent efforts on Dost Mahomed's part availed to expel the Sikhs from Peshawur, and suspicious of British connivance with Runjeet Singh's successful aggression, he took into consideration the policy of fortifying himself by a counter alliance with Persia. As for Shah Soojah, he had crept back to his refuge at Loodianah.

Lord Auckland succeeded Lord William Bentinck as Governor-General of India in March 1836. In reply to Dost Mahomed's letter of congratulation, his lordship wrote: 'You are aware that it is not the practice of the British Government to interfere with the affairs of other independent states;' an abstention which Lord Auckland was soon to violate. He had brought from England the feeling of disquietude in regard to the designs of Persia and Russia which the communications of our envoy in Persia had fostered in the Home Government, but it would appear that he was wholly undecided what line of action to pursue. 'Swayed,' says Durand, 'by the vague apprehensions of a remote danger entertained by others rather than himself,' he despatched to Afghanistan Captain Burnes on a nominally commercial mission, which, in fact, was one of political discovery, but without definite instructions. Burnes, an able but rash and ambitious man, reached Cabul in September 1837, two months before the Persian army began the siege of Herat. He had a strong prepossession in favour of the Dost, whose guest he had already been in 1832, and the policy he favoured was not the revival of the legitimate dynasty in the person of Shah Soojah, but the attachment of Dost Mahomed to British interests by strengthening his throne and affording him British countenance.

Burnes sanguinely believed that he had arrived at Cabul in the nick of time, for an envoy from the Shah of Persia was already at Candahar, bearing presents and assurances of support. The Dost made no concealment to Burnes of his approaches to Persia and Russia, in despair of British good offices, and being hungry for assistance from any source to meet the encroachments of the Sikhs, he professed himself ready to abandon his negotiations with the western powers if he were given reason to expect countenance and assistance at the hands of the Anglo-Indian Government. Burnes communicated to his Government those friendly proposals, supporting them by his own strong representations, and meanwhile, carried away by enthusiasm, he exceeded his powers by making efforts to dissuade the Candahar chiefs from the Persian alliance, and by offering to support them with money to enable them to make head against the offensive, by which Persia would probably seek to revenge the rejection of her overtures. For this unauthorised excess of zeal Burnes was severely reprimanded by his Government, and was directed to retract his offers to the Candahar chiefs. The situation of Burnes in relation to the Dost was presently complicated by the arrival at Cabul of a Russian officer claiming to be an envoy from the Czar, whose credentials, however, were regarded as dubious, and who, if that circumstance has the least weight, was on his return to

Russia utterly repudiated by Count Nesselrode. The Dost took small account of this emissary, continuing to assure Burnes that he cared for no connection except with the English, and Burnes professed to his Government his fullest confidences in the sincerity of those declarations. But the tone of Lord Auckland's reply, addressed to the Dost, was so dictatorial and supercilious as to indicate the writer's intention that it should give offence. It had that effect, and Burnes' mission at once became hopeless. Yet, as a last resort, Dost Mahomed lowered his pride so far as to write to the Governor-General imploring him 'to remedy the grievances of the Afghans, and afford them some little encouragement and power.' The pathetic representation had no effect. The Russian envoy, who was profuse in his promises of everything which the Dost was most anxious to obtain, was received into favour and treated with distinction, and on his return journey he effected a treaty with the Candahar chiefs, which was presently ratified by the Russian minister at the Persian Court. Burnes, fallen into discredit at Cabul, quitted that place in August 1838. He had not been discreet, but it was not his indiscretion that brought about the failure of his mission. A nefarious transaction, which Kaye denounces with the passion of a just indignation, connects itself with Burnes' negotiations with the Dost; his official correspondence was unscrupulously mutilated and garbled in the published Blue Book with deliberate purpose to deceive the British public.

Burnes had failed because, since he had quitted India for Cabul, Lord Auckland's policy had gradually altered. Lord Auckland had landed in India in the character of a man of peace. That, so late as April 1837, he had no design of obstructing the existing situation in Afghanistan is proved by his written statement of that date, that 'the British Government had resolved decidedly to discourage the prosecution by the ex-king Shah Soojah-ool-Moolk, so long as he may remain under our protection, of further schemes of hostility against the chiefs now in power in Cabul and Candahar.' Yet, in the following June, he concluded a treaty which sent Shah Soojah to Cabul, escorted by British bayonets. Of this inconsistency no explanation presents itself. It was a far cry from our frontier on the Sutlej to Herat in the confines of Central Asia—a distance of more than 1200 miles, over some of the most arduous marching ground in the known world. No doubt the Anglo-Indian Government was justified in being somewhat concerned by the facts that a Persian army, backed by Russian volunteers and Russian roubles, was besieging Herat, and that Persian and Russian emissaries were at work in Afghanistan. Both phenomena were rather of the 'bogey' character; how much so to-day shows when the Afghan frontier is still beyond Herat, and when a descendant of Dost Mahomed still sits in the Cabul musnid . But neither England nor India scrupled to make the Karrack counter-threat which arrested the siege of Herat; and the obvious policy as regarded Afghanistan was to watch the results of the intrigues which were on foot, to ignore them should they come to nothing, as was probable, to counteract them by familiar methods if serious consequences should seem impending. Our alliance with Runjeet Singh was solid, and the quarrel between Dost Mahomed and him concerning the Peshawur province was notoriously easy of arrangement.

On whose memory rests the dark shadow of responsibility for the first Afghan war? The late Lord Broughton, who, when Sir John Cam Hobhouse, was President of the Board of Control from 1835 to 1841, declared before a House of Commons Committee, in 1851, 'The Afghan war was done by myself; entirely without the privity of the Board of Directors.' The meaning of that declaration, of course, was that it was the British Government of the day which was responsible, acting through its member charged with the control of Indian affairs; and further, that the directorate of the East India Company was accorded no voice in the matter. But this utterance was materially qualified by Sir J. C. Hobhouse's statement in the House of Commons in 1842, that his despatch indicating the policy to be adopted, and that written by Lord Auckland, informing him that the expedition had already been undertaken, had crossed each other on the way.

It would be tedious to detail how Lord Auckland, under evil counsel, gradually boxed the compass from peace to war. The scheme of action embodied in the treaty which, in the early summer of 1838, was concluded between the Anglo-Indian Government, Runjeet Singh, and Shah Soojah, was that Shah Soojah, with a force officered from an Indian army, and paid by British money, possessing also the good-will and support of the Maharaja of the Punjaub, should attempt the recovery of his throne without any stiffening of British bayonets at his back. Then it was urged, and the representation was indeed accepted, that the Shah would need the buttress afforded by English troops, and that a couple of regiments only would suffice to afford this prestige. But Sir Harry Fane, the Commander-in-Chief, judiciously interposed his veto on the despatch of a handful of British soldiers on so distant and hazardous an expedition. Finally, the Governor-General, committed already to a mistaken line of policy, and urged forward by those about him, took the unfortunate resolution to gather together an Anglo-Indian army, and to send it, with the ill-omened Shah Soojah on its shoulders, into the unknown and distant wilds of Afghanistan. This action determined on, it was in accordance with the Anglo-Indian fitness of things that the Governor-General should promulgate a justificatory manifesto. Of this composition it is unnecessary to say more than to quote Durand's observation that in it 'the words "justice and necessity" were applied in a manner for which there is fortunately no precedent in the English language,' and Sir Henry Edwardes' not less trenchant comment that 'the views and conduct of Dost Mahomed were misrepresented with a hardihood which a Russian statesman might have envied.'

All men whose experience gave weight to their words opposed this 'preposterous enterprise.' Mr Elphinstone, who had been the head of a mission to Cabul thirty years earlier, held that 'if an army was sent up the passes, and if we could feed it, no doubt we might take Cabul and set up Shah Soojah; but it was hopeless to maintain him in a poor, cold, strong and remote country, among so turbulent a people.' Lord William Bentinck, Lord Auckland's predecessor, denounced the project as an act of incredible folly. Marquis Wellesley regarded 'this wild expedition into a distant region of rocks and deserts, of sands and ice and snow,' as an act of infatuation. The Duke of Wellington pronounced with prophetic sagacity, that the consequence of once crossing the Indus to settle a government in Afghanistan would be a perennial march into that country.

CHAPTER 2

The March to Cabul

The two main objects of the venturesome offensive movement to which Lord Auckland had committed himself were, first, the raising of the Persian siege of Herat if the place should hold out until reached—the recapture of it if it should have fallen; and, secondly, the establishment of Shah Soojah on the Afghan throne. The former object was the more pressing, and time was very precious; but the distances in India are great, the means of communication in 1838 did not admit of celerity, and the seasons control the safe prosecution of military operations. Nevertheless, the concentration of the army at the frontier station of Ferozepore was fully accomplished toward the end of November. Sir Harry Fane was to be the military head of the expedition, and he had just right to be proud of the 14,000 carefully selected and well-seasoned troops who constituted his Bengal contingent. The force consisted of two infantry divisions, of which the first, commanded by Major-General Sir Willoughby Cotton, contained three brigades, commanded respectively by Colonels Sale, Nott, and Dennis, of whom the two former were to attain high distinction within the borders of Afghanistan. Major-General Duncan commanded the second infantry division of the two brigades, of which one was commanded by Colonel Roberts, the gallant father of a gallant son, the other by

Colonel Worsley. The 6000 troops raised for Shah Soojah, who were under Fane's orders, and were officered from our army in India, had been recently and hurriedly recruited, and although rapidly improving, were not yet in a state of high efficiency. The contingent which the Bombay Presidency was to furnish to the 'Army of the Indus,' and which landed about the close of the year near the mouth of the Indus, was under the command of General Sir John Keane, the Commander-in-Chief of the Bombay army. The Bombay force was about 5000 strong.

Before the concentration at Ferozepore had been completed, Lord Auckland received official intimation of the retreat of the Persians from before Herat. With their departure had gone, also, the sole legitimate object of the expedition; there remained but a project of wanton aggression and usurpation. The Russo-Persian failure at Herat was scarcely calculated to maintain in the astute and practical Afghans any hope of fulfilment of the promises which the western powers had thrown about so lavishly, while it made clear that, for some time at least to come, the Persians would not be found dancing again to Russian fiddling. The abandonment of the siege of Herat rendered the invasion of Afghanistan an aggression destitute even of pretext. The Governor-General endeavoured to justify his resolution to persevere in it by putting forth the argument that its prosecution was required, 'alike in observation of the treaties entered into with Runjeet Singh and Shah Soojah as by paramount considerations of defensive policy.' A remarkable illustration of 'defensive policy' to take the offensive against a remote country from whose further confines had faded away foiled aggression, leaving behind nothing but a bitter consciousness of broken promises! As for the other plea, the tripartite treaty contained no covenant that we should send a corporal's guard across our frontier. If Shah Soojah had a powerful following in Afghanistan, he could regain his throne without our assistance; if he had no holding there, it was for us a truly discreditable enterprise to foist him on a recalcitrant people at the point of the bayonet.

One result of the tidings from Herat was to reduce by a division the strength of the expeditionary force. Fane, who had never taken kindly to the project, declined to associate himself with the diminished array that remained. The command of the Bengal column fell to Sir Willoughby Cotton, with whom as his aide-de-camp rode that Henry Havelock whose name twenty years later was to ring through India and England. Duncan's division was to stand fast at Ferozepore as a support, by which disposition the strength of the Bengal marching force was cut down to about 9500 fighting men. After its junction with the Bombay column, the army would be 14,500 strong, without reckoning the Shah's contingent. There was an interlude at Ferozepore of reviews and high jinks with the shrewd, debauched old Runjeet Singh; of which proceedings Havelock in his narrative of the expedition gives a detailed account, dwelling with extreme disapprobation on Runjeet's addiction to a 'pet tipple' strong enough to lay out the hardest drinker in the British camp, but which the old reprobate quaffed freely without turning a hair.

At length, on December 10th, 1838, Cotton began the long march which was not to terminate at Cabul until August 6th of the following year. The most direct route was across the Punjaub, and up the passes from Peshawur, but the Governor-General had shrunk from proposing to Runjeet Singh that the force should march through his territories, thinking it enough that the Maharaja had permitted Shah Soojah's heir, Prince Timour, to go by Peshawur to Cabul, had engaged to support him with a Sikh force, and had agreed to maintain an army of reserve at Peshawur.

The chosen route was by the left bank of the Sutlej to its junction with the Indus, down the left bank of the Indus to the crossing point at Roree, and from Sukkur across the Scinde and northern Belooch provinces by the Bolan and Kojuk passes to Candahar, thence by Khelat-i-Ghilzai and Ghuznee to Cabul. This was a line excessively circuitous, immensely long, full of difficulties, and equally disadvantageous as to supplies and communications. On the way the column would have to effect a junction with the Bombay force, which at Vikkur was distant 800 miles from Ferozepore. Of the distance of 850 miles from the latter post to Candahar the first half to the crossing of the Indus presented no serious difficulties, but from Sukkur beyond the country was inhospitable and cruelly rugged. It needed little military knowledge to realise how more and yet more precarious would become the communications as the chain lengthened, to discern that from Ferozepore to the Indus they would be at the mercy of the Sikhs, and to comprehend this also, that a single serious check, in or beyond the passes, would involve all but inevitable ruin.

Shah Soojah and his levies moved independently some marches in advance of Cotton. The Dooranee monarch-elect had already crossed the Indus, and was encamped at Shikarpore, when he was joined by Mr William Hay Macnaghten, of the Company's Civil Service, the high functionary who had been gazetted as 'Envoy and Minister on the part of the Government of India at the Court of Shah Soojah-ool-Moolk.' Durand pronounces the selection an unhappy one, 'for Macnaghten, long accustomed to irresponsible office, inexperienced in men, and ignorant of the country and people of Afghanistan, was, though an erudite Arabic scholar, neither practised in the field of Asiatic intrigue nor a man of action. His ambition was, however, great, and the expedition, holding out the promise of distinction and honours, had met with his strenuous advocacy.' Macnaghten was one of the three men who chiefly inspired Lord Auckland with the policy to which he had committed himself. He was the negotiator of the tripartite treaty. He was now on his way toward a region wherein he was to concern himself in strange adventures, the outcome of which was to darken his reputation, consign him to a sudden cruel death, bring awful ruin on the enterprise he had fostered, and inflict incalculable damage on British prestige in India.

Marching through Bhawulpore and Northern Scinde, without noteworthy incident save heavy losses of draught cattle, Cotton's army reached Roree, the point at which the Indus was to be crossed, in the third week of January 1839. Here a delay was encountered. The Scinde Ameers were, with reason, angered by the unjust and exacting terms which Pottinger had been instructed to enforce on them. They had been virtually independent of Afghanistan for nearly half a century; there was now masterfully demanded of them quarter of a million sterling in name of back tribute, and this in the face of the fact that they held a solemn release by Shah Soojah of all past and future claims. When they demurred to this, and to other exactions, they were peremptorily told that 'neither the ready power to crush and annihilate them, nor the will to call it into action, was wanting if it appeared requisite, however remotely, for the safety and integrity of the Anglo-Indian empire and frontier.'

It was little wonder that the Ameers were reluctant to fall in with terms advanced so arrogantly. Keane marched up the right bank of the Indus to within a couple of marches of Hyderabad, and having heard of the rejection by the Ameers of Pottinger's terms, and of the gathering of some 20,000 armed Belooches about the capital, he called for the co-operation of part of the Bengal column in a movement on Hyderabad. Cotton started on his march down the left bank, on January Jeth, with 5600 men. Under menaces so ominous the unfortunate Ameers succumbed. Cotton returned to Roree; the Bengal column crossed the Indus, and on February 20th its headquarters reached Shikarpore. Ten days later, Cotton, leading the advance, was in Dadur, at the foot of the Bolan Pass, having suffered heavily in transport animals almost from the start. Supplies were scarce in a region so barren, but with a month's partial food on his beasts of burden he quitted Dadur March 10th, got safely, if toilsomely, through the Bolan, and on 26th reached Quetta, where he was to halt for orders. Shah Soojah and Keane followed, their troops suffering not a little from scarcity of supplies and loss of animals.

Keane's error in detaining Cotton at Quetta until he should arrive proved itself in the semi-starvation to which the troops of the Bengal column were reduced. The Khan of Khelat, whether from disaffection or inability, left unfulfilled his promise to supply grain, and the result of the quarrel which Burnes picked with him was that he shunned coming in and paying homage to Shah Soojah, for which default he was to suffer cruel and unjustifiable ruin. The sepoys were put on half, the camp followers on quarter rations, and the force for eleven days had been idly consuming the waning supplies, when at length, on April 6th, Keane came into camp, having already formally assumed the command of the whole army, and made certain alterations in its organisation and subsidiary commands. There still remained to be traversed 147 miles before Candahar should be reached, and the dreaded Kojuk Pass had still to be penetrated.

Keane was a soldier who had gained a reputation for courage in Egypt and the Peninsula. He was indebted to the acuteness of his engineer and the valour of his troops, for the peerage conferred on him for Ghuznee, and it cannot be said that during his command in Afghanistan he disclosed any marked military aptitude. But he had sufficient perception to recognise that he had brought the Bengal column to the verge of starvation in Quetta, and sufficient common sense to discern that, since if it remained there it would soon starve outright, the best thing to be done was to push it forward with all possible speed into a region where food should be procurable. Acting on this reasoning, he marched the day after his arrival. Cotton, while lying in Quetta, had not taken the trouble to reconnoitre the passes in advance, far less to make a practicable road through the Kojuk defile if that should prove the best route. The resolution taken to march through it, two days were spent in making the pass possible for wheels; and from the 13th to the 21st the column was engaged in overcoming the obstacles it presented, losing in the task, besides, much baggage, supplies, transport and ordnance stores. Further back in the Bolan Willshire with the Bombay column was faring worse; he was plundered severely by tribal marauders.

By May 4th the main body of the army was encamped in the plain of Candahar. From the Kojuk, Shah Soojah and his contingent had led the advance toward the southern capital of the dominions from the throne of which he had been cast down thirty years before. The Candahar chiefs had meditated a night attack on his raw troops, but Macnaghten's intrigues and bribes had wrought defection in their camp; and while Kohun-dil-Khan and his brothers were in flight to Girishk on the Helmund, the infamous Hadji Khan Kakur led the venal herd of turncoat sycophants to the feet of the claimant who came backed by the British gold, which Macnaghten was scattering abroad with lavish hand. Shah Soojah recovered from his trepidation, hurried forward in advance of his troops, and entered Candahar on

THE BOLAN PASS

April 24th. His reception was cold. The influential chiefs stood aloof, abiding the signs of the times; the populace of Candahar stood silent and lowering. Nor did the sullenness abate when the presence of a large army with its followers promptly raised the price of grain, to the great distress of the poor. The ceremony of the solemn recognition of the Shah, held close to the scene of his defeat in 1834, Havelock describes as an imposing pageant, with homagings and royal salutes, parade of troops and presentation of nuzzurs ; but the arena set apart for the inhabitants was empty, spite of Eastern love for a tamasha , and the display of enthusiasm was confined to the immediate retainers of His Majesty.

The Shah was eager for the pursuit of the fugitive chiefs; but the troops were jaded and sickly, the cavalry were partially dismounted, and what horses remained were feeble skeletons. The transport animals needed grazing and rest, and their loss of numbers to be made good. The crops were not yet ripe, and provisions were scant and dear. When, on May 9th, Sale marched toward Girishk, his detachment carried half rations, and his handful of regular cavalry was all that two regiments could furnish. Reaching Girishk, he found that the chiefs had fled toward Seistan, and leaving a regiment of the Shah's contingent in occupation, he returned to Candahar.

Macnaghten professed the belief, and perhaps may have deluded himself into it, that Candahar had received the Shah with enthusiasm. He was sanguine that the march to Cabul would be unopposed, and he urged on Keane, who was wholly dependent on the Envoy for political information, to move forward at once, lightening the difficulties of the march by leaving the Bombay troops at Candahar. But Keane declined, on the advice of Thomson, his chief engineer, who asked significantly whether he had found the information given him by the political department in any single instance correct. Food prospects, however, did not improve at Candahar, and leaving a strong garrison there as well, curious to say, as the siege train which with arduous labour had been brought up the passes, Keane began the march to Cabul on June 27th. He had supplies only sufficient to carry his army thither on half rations. Macnaghten had lavished money so freely that the treasury chest was all but empty. How the Afghans regarded the invasion was evinced by condign slaughter of our stragglers.

As the army advanced up the valley of the Turnuk, the climate became more temperate, the harvest was later, and the troops improved in health and spirit. Concentrating his forces, Keane reached Ghuznee on July 21st. The reconnaissance he made proved that fortress occupied in force. The outposts driven in, and a close inspection made, the works were found stronger than had been represented, and its regular reduction was out of the question without the battering train which Keane had allowed himself to be persuaded into leaving behind. A wall some 70 feet high and a wet ditch in its front made mining and escalade alike impracticable. Thomson, however, noticed that the road and bridge to the Cabul gate were intact. He obtained trustworthy information that up to a recent date, while all the other gates had been built up, the Cabul gate had not been so dealt with. As he watched, a horseman was seen to enter by it. This was conclusive. The ground within 400 yards of the gate offered good artillery positions. Thomson therefore reported that although the operation was full of risk, and success if attained must cost dear, yet in the absence of a less hazardous method of reduction there offered a fair chance of success in an attempt to blow open the Cabul gate, and then carry the place by a coup de main . Keane was precluded from the alternative of masking the place and continuing his advance by the all but total exhaustion of his supplies, which the capture of Ghuznee would replenish, and he therefore resolved on an assault by the Cabul gate.

During the 21st July the army circled round the place, and camped to the north of it on the Cabul road. The following day was spent in preparations, and in defeating an attack made on the Shah's contingent by several thousand Ghilzai tribesmen of the adjacent hill country. In the gusty darkness of the early morning of the 23d the field artillery was placed in battery on the heights opposite the northern face of the fortress. The 13th regiment was extended in skirmishing order in the gardens under the wall of this face, and a detachment of sepoys was detailed to make a false attack on the eastern face. Near the centre of the northern face was the Cabul gate, in front of which lay waiting for the signal, a storming party consisting of the light companies of the four European regiments, under command of Colonel Dennie of the 13th. The main column consisted of two European regiments and the support of a third, the whole commanded by Brigadier Sale; the native regiments constituted the reserve. All those dispositions were completed by three A.M., and, favoured by the noise of the wind and the darkness, without alarming the garrison.

Punctually at this hour the little party of engineers charged with the task of blowing in the gate started forward on the hazardous errand. Captain Peat of the Bombay Engineers was in command. Durand, a young lieutenant of Bengal Engineers, who was later to attain high distinction, was entrusted with the service of heading the explosion party. The latter, leading the party, had advanced unmolested to within 150 yards of the works, when a challenge, a shot and a shout gave intimation of his detection. A musketry fire was promptly opened by the garrison from the battlements, and blue lights illuminated the

29

approach to the gate, but in the fortunate absence of fire from the lower works the bridge was safely crossed, and Peat with his handful of linesmen halted in a sallyport to cover the explosion operation. Durand advanced to the gate, his sappers piled their powder bags against it and withdrew; Durand and his sergeant uncoiled the hose, ignited the quick-match under a rain from the battlements of bullets and miscellaneous missiles, and then retired to cover out of reach of the explosion.

At the sound of the first shot from the battlements, Keane's cannon had opened their fire. The skirmishers in the gardens engaged in a brisk fusillade. The rattle of Hay's musketry was heard from the east. The garrison was alert in its reply. The northern ramparts became a sheet of flame, and everywhere the cannonade and musketry fire waxed in noise and volume. Suddenly, as the day was beginning to dawn, a dull, heavy sound was heard by the head of the waiting column, scarce audible elsewhere because of the boisterous wind and the din of the firing. A pillar of black smoke shot up from where had been the Afghan gate, now shattered by the 300 pounds of gunpowder which Durand had exploded against it. The signal to the storming party was to be the 'advance' sounded by the bugler who accompanied Peat. But the bugler had been shot through the head. Durand could not find Peat. Going back through the bullets to the nearest party of infantry, he experienced some delay, but at last the column was apprised that all was right, the 'advance' was sounded, Dennie and his stormers sped forward, and Sale followed at the head of the main column.

After a temporary check to the latter, because of a misconception, it pushed on in close support of Dennie. That gallant soldier and his gallant followers had rushed into the smoking and gloomy archway to find themselves met hand to hand by the Afghan defenders, who had recovered from their surprise. Nothing could be distinctly seen in the narrow gorge, but the clash of sword blade against bayonet was heard on every side. The stormers had to grope their way between the yet standing walls in a dusk which the glimmer of the blue light only made more perplexing. But some elbow room was gradually gained, and then, since there was neither time nor space for methodic street fighting, each loaded section gave its volley and then made way for the next, which, crowding to the front, poured a deadly discharge at half pistol-shot into the densely crowded defenders. Thus the storming party won steadily its way, till at length Dennie and his leading files discerned over the heads of their opponents a patch of blue sky and a twinkling star or two, and with a final charge found themselves within the place.

A body of fierce Afghan swordsmen projected themselves into the interval between the storming party and the main column. Sale, at the head of the latter, was cut down by a tulwar stroke in the face; in the effort of his blow the assailant fell with the assailed, and they rolled together among the shattered timbers of the gate. Sale, wounded again on the ground, and faint with loss of blood, called to one of his officers for assistance. Kershaw ran the Afghan through the body with his sword; but he still struggled with the Brigadier. At length in the grapple Sale got uppermost, and then he dealt his adversary a sabre cut which cleft him from crown to eyebrows. There was much confused fighting within the place, for the Afghan garrison made furious rallies again and again; but the citadel was found open and undefended, and by sunrise British banners were waving above its battlements Hyder Khan, the Governor of Ghuznee, one of the sons of Dost Mahomed, was found concealed in a house in the town and taken prisoner. The British loss amounted to about 200 killed and wounded, that of the garrison, which was estimated at from 3000 to 4000 strong, was over 500 killed. The number of wounded was not ascertained; of prisoners taken in arms there were about 1600. The booty consisted of numerous horses, camels and mules, ordnance and military weapons of various descriptions, and a vast quantity of supplies of all kinds.

Keane, having garrisoned Ghuznee, and left there his sick and wounded, resumed on July 30th his march on Cabul. Within twenty-four hours after the event Dost Mahomed heard of the fall of Ghuznee. Possessed of the adverse intelligence, the Dost gathered his chiefs, received their facile assurances of fidelity, sent his brother the Nawaub Jubbar Khan to ask what terms Shah Soojah and his British allies were prepared to offer him, and recalled from Jellalabad his son Akbar Khan, with all the force he could muster there. The Dost's emissary to the allied camp was informed that 'an honourable asylum' in British India was at the service of his brother; an offer which Jubbar Khan declined in his name without thanks. Before he left to share the fortunes of the Dost, the Sirdar is reported to have asked Macnaghten, 'If Shah Soojah is really our king, what need has he of your army and name? You have brought him here,' he continued, 'with your money and arms. Well, leave him now with us Afghans, and let him rule us if he can.' When Jubbar Khan returned to Cabul with his sombre message, the Dost, having been joined by Akbar Khan, concentrated his army, and found himself at the head of 13,000 men, with thirty guns; but he mournfully realised that he could lean no reliance on the constancy and courage of his adherents. Nevertheless, he marched out along the Ghuznee road, and drew up his force at Urgundeh, where he commanded the most direct line of retreat toward the western hill country of Bamian, in case his people would not fight, or should they fight, if they were beaten.

There was no fight in his following; scarcely, indeed, was there a loyal supporter among all those who had eaten his salt for years. There was true manhood in this chief whom we were replacing by an effete puppet. The Dost, Koran in hand, rode among his perfidious troops, and conjured them in the name of God and the Prophet not to dishonour themselves by transferring their allegiance to one who had filled Afghanistan with infidels and blasphemers. 'If,' he continued, 'you are resolved to be traitors to me, at least enable me to die with honour. Support the brother of Futteh Khan in one last charge against these Feringhee dogs. In that charge he will fall; then go and make your own terms with Shah Soojah.' The high-souled appeal inspired no worthy response; but one is loth to credit the testimony of the soldier-of-fortune Harlan that his guards forsook the Dost, and that the rabble of troops plundered his pavilion, snatched from under him the pillows of his divan, seized his prayer carpet, and finally hacked into pieces the tent and its appurtenances. On the evening of August 2d the hapless man shook the dust of the camp of traitors from his feet, and rode away toward Bamian, his son Akbar Khan, with a handful of resolute men, covering the retreat of his father and his family. Tidings of the flight of Dost Mahomed reached Keane on the 3d, at Sheikabad, where he had halted to concentrate; and Outram volunteered to head a pursuing party, to consist of some British officers as volunteers, some cavalry and some Afghan horse. Hadji Khan Kakur, the earliest traitor of his race, undertook to act as guide. This man's devices of delay defeated Outram's fiery energy, perhaps in deceit, perhaps because he regarded it as lacking discretion. For Akbar Khan made a long halt on the crown of the pass, waiting to check any endeavour to press closely on his fugitive father, and it would have gone hard with Outram, with a few fagged horsemen at his back, if Hadji Khan had allowed him to overtake the resolute young Afghan chief. As Keane moved forward, there fell to him the guns which the Dost had left in the Urgundeh position. On August 6th he encamped close to Cabul; and on the following day Shah Soojah made his public entry into the capital which he had last seen thirty years previously. After so many years of vicissitude, adventure and intrigue, he was again on the throne of his ancestors, but placed there by the bayonets of the Government whose creature he was, an insult to the nation whom he had the insolence to call his people.

The entry, nevertheless, was a goodly spectacle enough. Shah Soojah, dazzling in coronet, jewelled girdle and bracelets, but with no Koh-i-noor now glittering on his forehead, bestrode a white charger, whose equipments gleamed with gold. By his side rode Macnaghten and Burnes; in the pageant were the principal officers of the British army. Sabres flashed in front of the procession, bayonets sparkled in its rear, as it wended its way through the great bazaar which Pollock was to destroy three years later, and along the tortuous street to the gate of the Balla Hissar. But neither the monarch nor his pageant kindled the enthusiasm in the Cabulees. There was no voice of welcome; the citizens did not care to trouble themselves so much as to make him a salaam, and they stared at the European strangers harder than at his restored majesty. There was a touch of pathos in the burst of eagerness to which the old man gave way as he reached the palace, ran through the gardens, visited the apartments, and commented on the neglect everywhere apparent. Shah Soojah was rather a poor creature, but he was by no means altogether destitute of good points, and far worse men than he were actors in the strange historical episode of which he was the figurehead. He was humane for an Afghan; he never was proved to have been untrue to us; he must have had some courage of a kind else he would never have remained in Cabul when our people left it, in the all but full assurance of the fate which presently overtook him as a matter of course. Havelock thus portrays him: 'A stout person of the middle height, his chin covered with a long thick and neatly trimmed beard, dyed black to conceal the encroachments of time. His manner toward the English is gentle, calm and dignified, without haughtiness, but his own subjects have invariably complained of his reception of them as cold and repulsive, even to rudeness. His complexion is darker than that of the generality of Afghans, and his features, if not decidedly handsome, are not the reverse of pleasing; but the expression of his countenance would betray to a skilful physiognomist that mixture of timidity and duplicity so often observable in the character of the higher order of men in Southern Asia.'

CHAPTER 3

The First Year of Occupation

Sir John Kaye, in his picturesque if diffuse history of the first Afghan war, lays it down that, in seating Shah Soojah on the Cabul throne, 'the British Government had done all that it had undertaken to do,' and Durand argues that, having accomplished this, 'the British army could have then been withdrawn with the honour and fame of entire success.' The facts apparently do not justify the reasoning of either writer. In the Simla manifesto, in which Lord Auckland embodied the rationale of his policy, he expressed the confident hope 'that the Shah will be speedily replaced on his throne by his own subjects and adherents, and when once he shall be received in power, and the independence and integrity of Afghanistan established, the British army will be withdrawn.' The Shah had been indeed restored to his throne, but by British bayonets, not by 'his own subjects and adherents.' It could not seriously be maintained that he was secure in power, or that the independence and integrity of Afghanistan were established when British troops were holding Candahar, Ghuznee and Cabul, the only three positions where the Shah was nominally paramount, when the fugitive Dost was still within its borders, when intrigue and disaffection were seething in every valley and on every hillside, and when the principality of Herat maintained a contemptuous independence. Macnaghten might avow himself convinced of the popularity of the Shah, and believe or strive to believe that the Afghans had received the puppet king `with feelings nearly amounting to adoration,' but he did not venture to support the conviction he avowed by advocating that the Shah should be abandoned to his adoring subjects. Lord Auckland's policy was gravely and radically erroneous, but it had a definite object, and that object certainly was not a futile march to Cabul and back, dropping incidentally by the wayside the aspirant to a throne whom he had himself put forward, and leaving him to take his chance among a truculent and adverse population. Thus early, in all probability, Lord Auckland was disillusioned of the expectation that the effective restoration of Shah Soojah would be of light and easy accomplishment, but at least he could not afford to have the enterprise a coup manqué when as yet it was little beyond its inception.

The cost of the expedition was already, however, a strain, and the troops engaged in it were needed in India. Lord Auckland intimated to Macnaghten his expectation that a strong brigade would suffice to hold Afghanistan in conjunction with the Shah's contingent, and his desire that the rest of the army of the Indus should at once return to India. Macnaghten, on the other hand, in spite of his avowal of the Shah's popularity, was anxious to retain in Afghanistan a large body of troops. He meditated strange enterprises, and proposed that Keane should support his project of sending a force toward Bokhara to give check to a Russian column which Pottinger at Herat had heard was assembling at Orenburg, with Khiva for its objective. Keane derided the proposal, and Macnaghten reluctantly abandoned it, but he demanded of Lord Auckland with success, the retention in Afghanistan of the Bengal division of the army. In the middle of September General Willshire marched with the Bombay column, with orders, on his way to the Indus to pay a hostile visit to Khelat, and punish its khan for the 'disloyalty' with which he had been charged, a commission which the British officer fulfilled with a skill and thoroughness that could be admired with less reservation had the aggression on the gallant Mehrab been less wanton. A month later Keane started for India by the Khyber route, which Wade had opened without serious resistance when in August and September he escorted through the passes Prince Timour, Shah Soojah's heir-apparent. During the temporary absence of Cotton, who accompanied Keane, Nott had the command at Candahar, Sale at and about Cabul, and the troops were quartered in those capitals, and in Jellalabad, Ghuznee, Charikar and Bamian. The Shah and the Envoy wintered in the milder climate of Jellalabad, and Burnes was in political charge of the capital and its vicinity.

It was a prophetic utterance that the accomplishment of our military succession would mark but the commencement of our real difficulties in Afghanistan. In theory and in name Shah Soojah was an independent monarch; it was, indeed, only in virtue of his proving himself able to rule independently that he could justify his claim to rule at all. But that he was independent was a contradiction in terms while British troops studded the country, and while the real powers of sovereignty were exercised by Macnaghten. Certain functions, it is true, the latter did permit the nominal monarch to exercise. While debarred from a voice in measures of external policy, and not allowed to sway the lines of conduct to be adopted toward independent or revolting tribes, the Shah was allowed to concern himself with the administration of justice, and in his hands were the settlement, collection and appropriation of the revenue of those portions of the kingdom from which any revenue could be exacted. He was allowed to appoint as his minister of state,

Khelat

the companion of his exile, old Moolla Shikore, who had lost both his memory and his ears, but who had sufficient faculty left to hate the English, to oppress the people, to be corrupt and venal beyond all conception, and to appoint subordinates as flagitious as himself. 'Bad ministers,' wrote Burnes,'are in every government solid ground for unpopularity; and I doubt if ever a king had a worse set than has Shah Soojah.'The oppressed people appealed to the British functionaries, who remonstrated with the minister, and the minister punished the people for appealing to the British functionaries. The Shah was free to confer grants of land on his creatures, but when the holders resisted, he was unable to enforce his will since he was not allowed to employ soldiers; and the odium of the forcible confiscation ultimately fell on Macnaghten, who alone had the ordering of expeditions, and who could not see the Shah belittled by non-fulfilment of his requisitions.

Justice sold by venal judges, oppression and corruption rampant in every department of internal administration, it was no wonder that nobles and people alike resented the inflictions under whose sting they writhed. They were accustomed to a certain amount of oppression; Dost Mahomed had chastised them with whips, but Shah Soojah, whom the English had brought, was chastising them with scorpions. And they felt his yoke the more bitterly because, with the shrewd acuteness of the race, they recognised the really servile condition of this new king. They fretted, too, under the sharp bit of the British political agents who were strewn about the country, in the execution of a miserable and futile policy, and whose lives, in a few instances, did not maintain the good name of their country. Dost Mahomed had maintained his sway by politic management of the chiefs, and through them of the tribes. Macnaghten would have done well to impress on Shah Soojah the wisdom of pursuing the same tactics. There was, it is true, the alternative of destroying the power of the barons, but that policy involved a stubborn and doubtful struggle, and prolonged occupation of the country by British troops in great strength. Macnaghten professed our occupation of Afghanistan to be temporary; yet he was clearly adventuring on the rash experiment of weakening the nobles when he set about the enlistment of local tribal levies, who, paid from the Royal treasury and commanded by British officers, were expected to be staunch to the Shah, and useful in curbing the powers of the chiefs. The latter, of course, were alienated and resentful, and the levies, imbued with the Afghan attribute of fickleness, proved for the most part undisciplined and faithless.

The winter of 1839-40 passed without much noteworthy incident. The winter climate of Afghanistan is severe, and the Afghan, in ordinary circumstances, is among the hibernating animals. But down in the Khyber, in October, the tribes gave some trouble. They were dissatisfied with the amount of annual black-mail paid them for the right of way through their passes. When the Shah was a fugitive thirty years previously, they had concealed and protected him; and mindful of their kindly services, he had promised them, unknown to Macnaghten, the augmentation of their subsidy to the old scale from which it had gradually dwindled. Wade, returning from Cabul, did not bring them the assurances they expected, whereupon they rose and concentrated and invested Ali Musjid, a fort which they regarded as the key of their gloomy defile. Mackeson, the Peshawur political officer, threw provisions and ammunition into Ali Musjid, but the force, on its return march, was attacked by the hillmen, the Sikhs being routed, and the sepoys incurring loss of men and transport. The emboldened Khyberees now turned on Ali

Musjid in earnest; but the garrison was strengthened, and the place was held until a couple of regiments marched down from Jellalabad, and were preparing to attack the hillmen, when it was announced that Mackeson had made a compact with the chiefs for the payment of an annual subsidy which they considered adequate.

Afghanistan fifty years ago, and the same is in a measure true of it to-day, was rather a bundle of provinces, some of which owned scarcely a nominal allegiance to the ruler in Cabul, than a concrete state. Herat and Candahar were wholly independent, the Ghilzai tribes inhabiting the wide tracts from the Suliman ranges westward beyond the road through Ghuznee, between Candahar and Cabul, and northward into the rugged country between Cabul and Jellalabad, acknowledged no other authority than that of their own chiefs. The Ghilzais are agriculturists, shepherds, and robbers; they are constantly engaged in internal feuds; they are jealous of their wild independence, and through the centuries have abated little of their untamed ferocity. They had rejected Macnaghten's advances, and had attacked Shah Soojah's camp on the day before the fall of Ghuznee. Outram, in reprisal, had promptly raided part of their country. Later, the winter had restrained them from activity, but they broke out again in the spring. In May Captain Anderson, marching from Candahar with a mixed force about 1200 strong, was offered battle near Jazee, in the Turnuk, by some 2000 Ghilzai horse and foot. Andersen's guns told heavily among the Ghilzai horsemen, who, impatient of the fire, made a spirited dash on his left flank. Grape and musketry checked them; but they rallied, and twice charged home on the bayonets before they withdrew, leaving 200 of their number dead on the ground. Nott sent a detachment to occupy the fortress of Khelat-i-Ghilzai, between Candahar and Ghuznee, thus rendering the communications more secure; and later, Macnaghten bribed the chiefs by an annual subsidy of £600 to abstain from infesting the highways. The terms were cheap, for the Ghilzai tribes mustered some 40,000 fighting men.

Shah Soojah and the Envoy returned from Jellalabad to Cabul in April 1840. A couple of regiments had wintered not uncomfortably in the Balla Hissar. That fortress was then the key of Cabul, and while our troops remained in Afghanistan it should not have been left ungarrisoned a single hour. The soldiers did their best to impress on Macnaghten the all-importance of the position. But the Shah objected to its continued occupation, and Macnaghten weakly yielded. Cotton, who had returned to the chief military command in Afghanistan, made no remonstrance; the Balla Hissar was evacuated, and the troops were quartered in cantonments built in an utterly defenceless position on the plain north of Cabul, a position whose environs were cumbered with walled gardens, and commanded by adjacent high ground, and by native forts which were neither demolished nor occupied. The troops, now in permanent and regularly constructed quarters, ceased to be an expeditionary force, and became substantially an army of occupation. The officers sent for their wives to inhabit with them the bungalows in which they had settled down. Lady Macnaghten, in the spacious mission residence which stood apart in its own grounds, presided over the society of the cantonments, which had all the cheery surroundings of the half-settled, half-nomadic life of our military people in the East. There were the 'coffee house' after the morning ride, the gathering round the bandstand in the evening, the impromptu dance, and the burra khana occasionally in the larger houses. A racecourse had been laid out, and there were 'sky' races and more formal meetings. And so 'as in the days that were before the flood, they were eating and drinking, and marrying and giving in marriage, and knew not until the flood came, and took them all away.'

Macnaghten engaged himself in a welter of internal and external intrigue, his mood swinging from singular complacency to a disquietude that sometimes approached despondency. It had come to be forced on him, in spite of his intermittent optimism, that the Government was a government of sentry-boxes, and that Afghanistan was not governed so much as garrisoned. The utter failure of the winter march attempted by Peroffski's Russian column across the frozen steppes on Khiva was a relief to him; but the state of affairs in Herat was a constant trouble and anxiety. Major Todd had been sent there as political agent, to make a treaty with Shah Kamran, and to superintend the repair and improvement of the fortifications of the city. Kamran was plenteously subsidised; he took Macnaghten's lakhs, but furtively maintained close relations with Persia. Detecting the double-dealing, Macnaghten urged on Lord Auckland the annexation of Herat to Shah Soojah's dominions, but was instructed to condone Kamran's duplicity, and try to bribe him higher. Kamran by no means objected to this policy, and, while continuing his intrigues with Persia, cheerfully accepted the money, arms and ammunition which Macnaghten supplied him with so profusely as to cause remonstrance on the part of the financial authorities in Calcutta. The Commander-in-Chief was strong enough to counteract the pressure which Macnaghten brought to bear on Lord Auckland in favour of an expedition against Herat, which his lordship at length finally negatived, to the great disgust of the Envoy, who wrote of the conduct of his chief as 'drivelling beyond contempt,' and 'sighed for a Wellesley or a Hastings.' The ultimate result of Macnaghten's negotiations with Shah Kamran was Major Todd's withdrawal from Herat. Todd had suspended the monthly subsidy, to the great wrath of Kamran's rapacious and treacherous minister Yar Mahomed, who made a peremptory demand for increased advances, and refused Todd's stipulation that a British force should be admitted into Herat. Todd's action in quitting Herat was severely censured by his superiors, and he was relegated to regimental duty. Perhaps he acted somewhat rashly, but he had not been kept well informed; for instance, he had been unaware that Persia had become our friend, and had engaged to cease relations with Shah Kamran—an important arrangement of which he certainly should have been cognisant. Macnaghten had squandered more gold on Herat than the fee-simple of the principality was worth, and to no purpose; he left that state just as he found it, treacherous, insolent, greedy and independent.

The precariousness of the long lines of communications between British India and the army in Afghanistan—a source of danger which from the first had disquieted cautious soldiers—was making itself seriously felt, and constituted for Macnaghten another cause of solicitude. Old Runjeet Singh, a faithful if not disinterested ally, had died on June 27th, 1839, the day on which Keane marched out from Candahar. The breath was scarcely out of the old reprobate when the Punjaub began to drift into anarchy. So far as the Sikh share in it was concerned, the tripartite treaty threatened to become a dead letter. The Lahore Durbar had not adequately fulfilled the undertaking to support Prince Timour's advance by the Khyber, nor was it duly regarding the obligation to maintain a force on the Peshawur frontier of the Punjaub. But those things were trivial in comparison with the growing reluctance manifested freely, to accord to our troops and convoys permission to traverse the Punjaub on the march to and from Cabul. The Anglo-Indian Government sent Mr Clerk to Lahore to settle the question as to the thoroughfare. He had instructions to be firm, and the Sikhs did not challenge Mr Clerk's stipulation that the Anglo-Indian Government must have unmolested right of way through the Punjaub, while he undertook to restrict the use of it as much as possible. This arrangement by no means satisfied the exacting Macnaghten, and he continued to worry himself by foreseeing all sorts of troublous contingencies unless measures were adopted for 'macadamising' the road through the Punjaub.

The summer of 1840 did not pass without serious interruptions to the British communications between Candahar and the Indus; nor without unexpected and ominous disasters before they were restored. General Willshire, with the returning Bombay column, had in the previous November stormed Mehrab Khan's ill-manned and worse armed fort of Khelat, and the Khan, disdaining to yield, had fallen in the hopeless struggle. His son Nusseer Khan had been put aside in favour of a collateral pretender, and became an active and dangerous malcontent. All Northern Beloochistan fell into a state of anarchy. A detachment of sepoys escorting supplies was cut to pieces in one of the passes. Quetta was attacked with great resolution by Nusseer Khan, but was opportunely relieved by a force sent from another post. Nusseer made himself master of Khelat, and there fell into his cruel hands Lieutenant Loveday, the British political officer stationed there, whom he treated with great barbarity, and finally murdered. A British detachment under Colonel Clibborn, was defeated by the Beloochees with heavy loss, and compelled to retreat. Nusseer Khan, descending into the low country of Cutch, assaulted the important post of Dadur, but was repulsed, and taking refuge in the hills, was routed by Colonel Marshall with a force from Kotree, whereupon he became a skulking fugitive. Nott marched down from Candahar with a strong force, occupied Khelat, and fully re-established communications with the line of the Indus, while fresh troops moved forward into Upper Scinde, and thence gradually advancing to Quetta and Candahar, materially strengthened the British position in Southern Afghanistan.

Dost Mahomed, after his flight from Cabul in 1839, had soon left the hospitable refuge afforded him in Khooloom, a territory west of the Hindoo Koosh beyond Bamian, and had gone to Bokhara on the treacherous invitation of its Ameer, who threw him into captivity. The Dost's family remained at Khooloom, in the charge of his brother Jubbar Khan. The advance of British forces beyond Bamian to Syghan and Bajgah, induced that Sirdar to commit himself and the ladies to British protection. Dr Lord, Macnaghten's political officer in the Bamian district, was a rash although well-meaning man. The errors he had committed since the opening of spring had occasioned disasters to the troops whose dispositions he controlled, and had incited the neighbouring hill tribes to active disaffection. In July Dost Mahomed made his escape from Bokhara, hurried to Khooloom, found its ruler and the tribes full of zeal for his cause, and rapidly grew in strength. Lord found it was time to call in his advance posts and concentrate at Bamian, losing in the operation an Afghan regiment which deserted to the Dost. Macnaghten reinforced Bamian, and sent Colonel Dennie to command there. On September 18th Dennie moved out with two guns and 800 men against the Dost's advance parties raiding in an adjacent valley. Those detachments driven back, Dennie suddenly found himself opposed to the irregular mass of Oosbeg horse and foot which constituted the army of the Dost. Mackenzie's cannon fire shook the undisciplined horde, the infantry pressed in to close quarters, and soon the nondescript host of the Dost was in panic flight, with Dennie's cavalry in eager pursuit. The Dost escaped with difficulty, with the loss of his entire personal equipment. He was once more a fugitive, and the Wali of Khooloom promptly submitted himself to the victors, and pledged himself to aid and harbour the broken chief no more. Macnaghten had been a prey to apprehension while the Dost's attitude was threatening; he was now in a glow of joy and hope.

But the Envoy's elation was short-lived. Dost Mahomed was yet to cause him much solicitude. Defeated in Bamian, he was ready for another attempt in the Kohistan country to the north of Cabul. Disaffection was rife everywhere throughout the kingdom, but it was perhaps most rife in the Kohistan, which was seething with intrigues in favour of Dost Mahomed, while the local chiefs were intensely exasperated by the exactions of the Shah's revenue collectors. Macnaghten summoned the chiefs to Cabul. They came, they did homage to the Shah and swore allegiance to him; they went away from the capital pledging each other to his overthrow, and jeering at the scantiness of the force they had seen at Cabul. Intercepted letters disclosed their schemes, and in the end of September Sale, with a considerable force, marched out to chastise the disaffected Kohistanees. The fort of Tootundurrah fell without resistance. Julgah, however, the next fort assailed, stubbornly held out, and officers and men fell in the unsuccessful attempt to storm it. In three weeks Sale marched to and fro through the Kohistan, pursuing will-o'-the-wisp rumours as to the whereabouts of the Dost, destroying forts on the course of his weary pilgrimage, and subjected occasionally to night attacks.

Meanwhile, in the belief that Dost Mahomed was close to Cabul, and mournfully conscious that the capital and surrounding country were ripe for a rising, Macnaghten had relapsed into nervousness, and was a prey to gloomy forebodings. The troops at Bamian were urgently recalled.

Cannon were mounted on the Balla Hissar to overawe the city, the concentration of the troops in the fortress was under consideration, and men were talking of preparing for a siege. How Macnaghten's English nature was undergoing deterioration under the strain of events is shown by his writing of the Dost: 'Would it be justifiable to set a price on this fellow's head?' How his perceptions were warped was further evinced by his talking of 'showing no mercy to the man who has been the author of all the evil now distracting the country,' and by his complaining of Sale and Burnes that, 'with 2000 good infantry, they are sitting down before a fortified place, and are afraid to attack it.'

Learning that for certain the Dost had crossed the Hindoo Koosh from Nijrao into the Kohistan, Sale, who had been reinforced, sent out reconnaissances which ascertained that he was in the Purwan Durrah valley, stretching down from the Hindoo Koosh to the Gorebund river; and the British force marched thither on 2d November. As the village was neared, the Dost's people were seen evacuating it and the adjacent forts, and making for the hills. Sale's cavalry was some distance in advance of the infantry of the advance guard, but time was precious. Anderson's horse went to the left, to cut off retreat down the Gorebund valley. Fraser took his two squadrons of Bengal cavalry to the right, advanced along the foothills, and gained the head of the valley. He was too late to intercept a small body of Afghan horsemen, who were already climbing the upland; but badly mounted as the latter were, he could pursue them with effect. But it seemed that the Afghans preferred to fight rather than be pursued. The Dost himself was in command of the little party, and the Dost was a man whose nature was to fight, not to run. He wheeled his handful so that his horsemen faced Fraser's troop down there below them. Then the Dost pointed to his banner, bared his head, called on his supporters in the name of God and the Prophet to follow him against the unbelievers, and led them down the slope.

Fraser had formed up his troopers when recall orders reached him. Joyous that the situation entitled him to disobey them, he gave instead the word to charge. As the Afghans came down at no great pace, they fired occasionally; either because of the bullets, or because of an access of pusillanimity, Fraser's troopers broke and fled ignominiously. The British gentlemen charged home unsupported. Broadfoot, Crispin and Lord were slain; Ponsonby, severely wounded and his reins cut, was carried out of the mêlée by his charger; Fraser, covered with blood and wounds, broke through his assailants, and brought to Sale his report of the disgrace of his troopers. After a sharp pursuit of the poltroons, the Dost and his followers leisurely quitted the field.

Burnes wrote to the Envoy—he was a soldier, but he was also a 'political,' and political employ seemed often in Afghanistan to deteriorate the attribute of soldierhood—that there was no alternative for the force but to fall back on Cabul, and entreated Macnaghten to order immediate concentration of all the troops. This letter Macnaghten received the day after the disaster in the Kohistan, when he was taking his afternoon ride in the Cabul plain. His heart must have been very heavy as he rode, when suddenly a horseman galloped up to him and announced that the Ameer was approaching. 'What Ameer?' asked Macnaghten. 'Dost Mahomed Khan,' was the reply, and sure enough there was the Dost close at hand. Dismounting, this Afghan prince and gentleman saluted the Envoy, and offered him his sword, which Macnaghten declined to take. Dost and Envoy rode into Cabul together, and such was the impression the former made on the latter that Macnaghten, who a month before had permitted himself to think of putting a price on 'the fellow's' head, begged now of the Governor-General 'that the Dost be treated more handsomely than was Shah Soojah, who had no claim on us.' And then followed a strange confession for the man to make who made the tripartite treaty, and approved the Simla manifesto: 'We had no hand in depriving the Shah of his kingdom, whereas we ejected the Dost, who never offended us, in support of our policy, of which he was the victim .'

Durand regards Dost Mahomed's surrender as 'evincing a strange pusillanimity.' This opprobrious judgment appears unjustified. No doubt he was weary of the fugitive life he had been leading, but to pronounce him afraid that the Kohistanees or any other Afghans would betray him is to ignore the fact that he had been for months among people who might, any hour of any day, have betrayed him if they had chosen. Nobler motives than those ascribed to him by Durand may be supposed to have actuated a man of his simple and lofty nature. He had given the arbitrament of war a trial, and had realised that in that way he could make no head against us. He might, indeed, have continued the futile struggle, but he was the sort of man to recognise the selfishness of that persistency which would involve ruin and death to the devoted people who would not desert his cause while he claimed to have a cause. When historians write of Afghan treachery and guile, it seems to have escaped their perception that Afghan treachery was but a phase of Afghan patriotism, of an unscrupulous character, doubtless, according to our notions, but nevertheless practical in its methods, and not wholly unsuccessful in its results. It may have been a higher and purer patriotism that moved Dost Mahomed to cease, by his surrender, from being an obstacle to the tranquillisation of the country of which he had been the ruler.

CHAPTER 4

The Second Year of Occupation

Dost Mahomed remained for a few days in the British cantonments on the Cabul plain, an honoured guest rather than a prisoner. His soldierly frankness, his bearing at once manly and courteous, his honest liking for and trust in our race, notwithstanding the experiences which he had undergone, won universal respect and cordiality. Officers who stood aloof from Shah Soojah vied with each other in evincing to Dost Mahomed their sympathy with him in his fallen fortunes. Shah Soojah would not see the man whom he had ingloriously supplanted, on the pretext that he 'could not bring himself to show common civility to such a villain.' How Macnaghten's feeling in regard to the two men had altered is disclosed by his comment on this refusal. 'It is well,' he wrote, 'as the Dost must have suffered much humiliation in being subjected to such an ordeal.'

In the middle of November 1840 the Dost began his journey toward British India, accompanied by Sir Willoughby Cotton, who was finally quitting Afghanistan, and under the escort of a considerable British force which had completed its tour of duty in Afghanistan. Sale succeeded Cotton in temporary divisional command pending the arrival of the latter's successor. About the middle of December Shah Soojah and his Court, accompanied by the British Envoy, arrived at Jellalabad for the winter, Burnes remaining at Cabul in political charge.

Macnaghten was mentally so constituted as to be continually alternating between high elation and the depths of despondency; discerning to-day ominous indications of ruin in an incident of no account, and to-morrow scorning imperiously to recognise danger in the fierce rising of a province. It may almost be said that each letter of his to Lord Auckland was of a different tone from the one which had preceded it. Burnes, who was nominally Macnaghten's chief lieutenant, with more self-restraint, had much the same temperament. Kaye writes of him: 'Sometimes sanguine, sometimes despondent, sometimes confident, sometimes credulous, Burnes gave to fleeting impressions all the importance and seeming permanency of settled convictions, and imbued surrounding objects with the colours of his own varying mind.' But if Burnes had been a discreet and steadfast man, he could have exercised no influence on the autocratic Macnaghten, since between the two men there was neither sympathy nor confidence. Burnes had, indeed, no specific duties of any kind; in his own words, he was in 'the most nondescript situation.' Macnaghten gave him no responsibility, and while Burnes waited for the promised reversion of the office of envoy, he chiefly employed himself in writing long memorials on the situation and prospects of affairs, on which Macnaghten's marginal comments were brusque, and occasionally contemptuous. The resolute and clear-headed Pottinger, who, if the opportunity had been given him, might have buttressed and steadied Macnaghten, was relegated to provincial service. Throughout his career in Afghanistan the Envoy could not look for much advice from the successive commanders of the Cabul force, even if he had cared to commune with them. Keane, indeed, did save him from the perpetration of one folly. But Cotton appears to have been a respectable nonentity. Sale was a stout, honest soldier, who was not fortunate on the only occasion which called him outside of his restricted métier. Poor Elphinstone was an object for pity rather than for censure.

It happened fortunately, in the impending misfortunes, that two men of stable temperament and lucid perception were in authority at Candahar. General Nott was a grand old Indian officer, in whom there was no guile, but a good deal of temper. He was not supple, and he had the habit of speaking his mind with great directness, a propensity which accounted, perhaps, for the repeated supersessions he had undergone. A clearheaded, shrewd man, he was disgusted with very many things which he recognised as unworthy in the conduct of the affairs of Afghanistan, and he was not the man to choose mild phrases in giving vent to his convictions. He had in full measure that chronic dislike which the Indian commander in the field nourishes to the political officer who is imposed on him by the authorities, and who controls his measures and trammels his actions. Nott's 'political,' who, the sole survivor of the men who were prominent during this unhappy period, still lives among us esteemed and revered, was certainly the ablest officer of the unpopular department to which he belonged; and how cool was Henry Rawlinson's temper is evinced in his ability to live in amity with the rugged and outspoken chief who addressed him in such a philippic as the following—words all the more trenchant because he to whom they were addressed must have realised how intrinsically true they were:—

'I have no right to interfere with the affairs of this country, and I never do so. But in reference to that part of your note where you speak of political influence, I will candidly tell you that these are not times for mere ceremony, and that under present circumstances, and at a distance of 2000 miles from the seat of the supreme Government, I throw responsibility to the wind, and tell you that in my opinion you have not had for some time past, nor have you at present, one particle of political influence in this country.'

Nott steadily laboured to maintain the morale and discipline of his troops, and thus watching the flowing tide of misrule and embroilment, he calmly made the best preparations in his power to meet the storm the sure and early outbreak of which his clear discernment prognosticated.

Shah Soojah's viceroy at Candahar was his heir-apparent Prince Timour. The Dooranee chiefs of Western Afghanistan had not unnaturally expected favours and influence under the rule of the Dooranee monarch; and while in Candahar before proceeding to Cabul, and still uncertain of what might occur there, Shah Soojah had been lavish of his promises. The chiefs had anticipated that they would be called around the vice-throne of Prince Timour; but Shah Soojah made the same error as that into which Louis XVIII. fell on his restoration. He constituted his Court of the men who had shared his Loodianah exile. The counsellors who went to Candahar with Timour were returned émigrés , in whom fitness for duty counted less than the qualification of companionship in exile. Those people had come back to Afghanistan poor; now they made haste to be rich by acts of oppressive injustice, in the exaction of revenue from the people, and by intercepting from the Dooranee chiefs the flow of royal bounty to which they had looked forward.

Uktar Khan was prominent among the Dooranee noblemen, and he had the double grievance of having been disappointed of the headship of the Zemindawar province on the western bank of the Helmund, and having been evilly entreated by the minions of Prince Timour. He had raised his clan and routed a force under a royalist follower, when Nott sent a detachment against him. Uktar Khan had crossed the Helmund into Zemindawar, when Farrington attacked him, and, after a brisk fight, routed and pursued him. The action was fought on January 3, 1841, in the very dead of winter; the intensity of the cold dispersed Uktar's levies, and Farrington returned to Candahar.

In reply to Macnaghten's demand for information regarding the origin of this outbreak, Rawlinson wrote him some home truths which were very distasteful. Rawlinson warned his chief earnestly of the danger which threatened the false position of the British in Afghanistan. He pointed out how cruel must be the revenue exactions which enabled Prince Timour's courtiers to absorb great sums. He expressed his suspicion that Shah Soojah had countenanced Uktar Khan's rising, and spoke of intrigues of dark and dangerous character. Macnaghten scouted Rawlinson's warning, and instructed him that 'it will make the consideration of all questions more simple if you will hereafter take for granted that as regards us "the king can do no wrong."' However, he and the Shah did remove from Candahar the Vakeel and his clique of obnoxious persons, who had been grinding the faces of the people; and the Envoy allowed himself to hope that this measure would restore order to the province of Candahar.

The hope was vain, the evil lay deeper; disaffection to the Shah and hatred to the British power were becoming intensified from day to day, and the aspiration for relief was swelling into a passion. In the days before our advent there had been venality and corruption in public places—occasionally, likely enough, as Macnaghten asserted, to an extent all but incredible. But exaction so sweeping could have occurred only in regions under complete domination; and in Afghanistan, even to this day, there are few regions wholly in this condition. When the yoke became over-weighty, a people of a nature so intractable knew how to resent oppression and oppose exaction. But now the tax gatherer swaggered over the land, and the people had to endure him, for at his back were the soldiers of the Feringhees and the levies of the Shah. The latter were paid by assignments on the revenues of specified districts; as the levies constituted a standing army of some size, the contributions demanded were heavier and more permanent than in bygone times. Macnaghten, aware of the discontent engendered by the system of assignments, desired to alter it. But the Shah's needs were pressing; the Anglo-Indian treasury was strained already by the expenditure in Afghanistan; and it was not easy in a period of turmoil and rebellion to carry out the amendment of a fiscal system. That, since the surrender of the Dost, there had been no serious rising in Northern or Eastern Afghanistan, sufficed to make Macnaghten an optimist of the moment. He had come by this time to a reluctant admission of the fact against which he had set his face so long, that Shah Soojah was unpopular. 'He has incurred,' he wrote, 'the odium that attaches to him from his alliance with us'; but the Envoy would not admit that our position in Afghanistan was a false one, in that we were maintaining by our bayonets, against the will of the Afghans, a sovereign whom they detested. 'It would,' he pleaded, 'be an act of downright dishonesty to desert His Majesty before he has found the means of taking root in the soil to which we have transplanted him.' While he wrote, Macnaghten must have experienced a sudden thrill of optimism or of self-delusion, for he continued: 'All things considered, the present tranquillity of this country is to my mind perfectly miraculous. Already our presence has been infinitely ben-

GHUZNEE

eficial in allaying animosities and in pointing out abuses.' If it had been the case that the country was tranquil, his adjective would have been singularly appropriate, but not precisely in the sense he meant to convey.

But there was no tranquillity, miraculous or otherwise. While Macnaghten was writing the letter which has just been quoted, Brigadier Shelton, who, about the New Year, had reached Jellalabad with a brigade from British India in relief of the force which was withdrawing with Cotton, was contending with an outbreak of the wild and lawless clans of the Khyber. When Macnaghten wrote, he had already received intelligence of the collapse of his projects in Herat, and that Major Todd, who had been his representative there, judging it imperative to break up the mission of which he was the head, had abruptly quitted that city, and was on his way to Candahar. Mischief was simmering in the Zemindawar country. The Ghilzai tribes of the region between Candahar and Ghuznee had accepted a subsidy to remain quiet, but the indomitable independence of this wild and fierce race was not to be tamed by bribes, and the spirit of hostility was manifesting itself so truculently that a British garrison had been placed in Khelat-i-Ghilzai, right in the heart of the disturbed territory. This warning and defensive measure the tribes had regarded with angry jealousy; but it was not until a rash 'political' had directed the unprovoked assault and capture of a Ghilzai fort that the tribes passionately flew to arms, bent on contesting the occupation of their rugged country. Colonel Wymer was sent from Candahar with a force, escorting a convoy of stores intended for the equipment of Khelat-i-Ghilzai. The tribes who had been loosely beleaguering that place marched down the Turnuk upon Wymer, and on May 19th attacked him with great impetuosity, under the command of a principal chief who was known as the 'Gooroo.' Wymer, in the protection of his convoy, had to stand on the defensive. The Ghilzais, regardless of the grape which tore through their masses, fell on sword in hand, and with an intuitive tactical perception struck Wymer simultaneously in front and flank. His sepoys had to change their dispositions, and the Ghilzais took the opportunity of their momentary dislocation to charge right home. They were met firmly by the bayonet, but again and again the hillmen renewed their attacks; and it was not till after five hours of hard fighting which cost them heavy loss, that at length, in the darkness, they suddenly drew off. Had they been Swiss peasants defending their mountains, or Poles struggling against the ferocious tyranny of Russia, their gallant effort might have excited praise and sympathy. Had they been Soudanese, a statesman might have spoken of them as a people 'rightly struggling to be free'; as it was, the Envoy vituperated them as 'a parcel of ragamuffins,' and Wymer's sepoys were held to have 'covered themselves with glory.' Macnaghten proceeded to encourage a sense of honour among the tribes by proposing the transfer to another chief, on condition of his seizing and delivering over the inconvenient 'Gooroo,' of the share of subsidy of which the latter had been in receipt.

While this creditable transaction was under consideration, Uktar Khan was again making himself very unpleasant; so much so that Macnaghten was authorising Rawlinson to offer a reward of 10,000 rupees for his capture, which accomplished, Rawlinson was instructed to 'hang the villain as high as Haman.' The gallows was not built, however, on which Uktar was to hang, although that chief sustained two severe defeats at the hands of troops sent from Candahar, and had to become a fugitive. The Ghilzais, who had gathered again after their defeat under the 'Gooroo,' had made little stand against the detachment which Colonel Chambers led out from Candahar, and they were again temporarily dispersed. The 'Gooroo' himself was in our hands. If the disaffection was in no degree diminished, the active ebullitions of it were assuredly quelled for the time. It was true, to be sure, that Akbar Khan, the fierce and resolute son of Dost Mahomed, had refused the Envoy's overtures to come in, and was wandering and plotting in Khooloom, quite ready to fulfil Macnaghten's prophetic apprehension that 'the fellow will be after some mischief should the opportunity present itself'; that the Dooranees were still defiant; that an insurgent force was out in the Dehrawat; and that the tameless chief Akram Khan was being blown from a gun by the cruel and feeble Timour. But unquestionably there was a comparative although short-lived lull in the overt hostility of the Afghan peoples against Shah Soojah and his foreign supporters; and Macnaghten characteristically announced that 'the country was quiet from Dan to Beersheba.' To one of his correspondents he wrote: 'From Mookoor to the Khyber Pass, all is content and tranquillity; and wherever we Europeans go, we are received with respect, attention and welcome. I think our prospects are most cheering; and with the materials we have there ought to be little or no difficulty in the management of the country. The people are perfect children, and they should be treated as such. If we put one naughty boy in the corner, the rest will be terrified.'

General Nott at Candahar, who 'never interfered in the government of the country,' but regarded the situation with shrewd, clear-headed common sense, differed utterly from the Envoy's view. The stout old soldier did not squander his fire; it was a close volley he discharged in the following words: 'The conduct of the thousand and one politicals has ruined our cause, and bared the throat of every European in this country to the sword and knife of the revengeful Afghan and bloody Belooch; and unless several regiments be quickly sent, not a man will be left to describe the fate of his comrades. Nothing will ever make the Afghans submit to the hated Shah Soojah, who is most certainly as great a scoundrel as ever lived.'

Nott's conclusions were in the main justified by after events, but the correctness of his premiss may be questioned. That the conduct of some of the political officers intensified the rancour of the Afghans is unhappily true, but the hate of our domination, and of the puppet thrust upon them by us, seems to have found its origin in a deeper feeling. The patriotism of a savage race is marked by features repulsive to civilised communities, but through the ruthless cruelty of the indiscriminate massacre, the treachery of the stealthy stab, and the lightly broken pledges, there may shine out the noblest virtue that a virile people can possess. A semi-barbarian nation whose manhood pours out its blood like water in stubborn resistance against an alien yoke, may be pardoned for many acts shocking to civilised communities which have not known the bitterness of stern and masterful subjugation.

CHAPTER 5

The Beginning of the End

The deceptive quietude of Afghanistan which followed the sharp lessons administered to the Dooranees and the Ghilzais was not seriously disturbed during the month of September 1841, and Macnaghten was in a full glow of cheerfulness. His services had been recognised by his appointment to the dignified and lucrative post of Governor of the Bombay Presidency, and he was looking forward to an early departure for a less harassing and tumultuous sphere of action than that in which he had been labouring for two troubled years. The belief that he would leave behind him a quiescent Afghanistan, and Shah Soojah firmly established on its throne, was the complement, to a proud and zealous man, of the satisfaction which his promotion afforded.

One distasteful task he had to perform before he should go. The Home Government had become seriously disquieted by the condition of affairs in Afghanistan. The Secret Committee of the Court of Directors, the channel through which the ministry communicated with the Governor-General, had expressed great concern at the heavy burden imposed on the Indian finances by the cost of the maintenance of the British force in Afghanistan, and by the lavish expenditure of the administration which Macnaghten directed. The Anglo-Indian Government was urgently required to review with great earnestness the question of its future policy in regard to Afghanistan, and to consider gravely whether an enterprise at once so costly and so unsatisfactory in results should not be frankly abandoned. Lord Auckland was alive to the difficulties and embarrassments which encompassed the position beyond the Indus, but he was loth to admit that the policy of which he had been the author, and in which the Home Government had abetted him so eagerly, was an utter failure. He and his advisers finally decided in favour of the continued occupation of Afghanistan; and since the Indian treasury was empty, and the annual charge of that occupation was not less than a million and a quarter sterling, recourse was had to a loan, Macnaghten was pressed to effect economies in the administration, and he was specially enjoined to cut down the subsidies which were paid to Afghan chiefs as bribes to keep them quiet. Macnaghten had objected to this retrenchment, pointing out that the stipends to the chiefs were simply compensation for the abandonment by them of their immemorial practice of highway robbery, but he yielded to pressure, called to Cabul the chiefs in its vicinity, and informed them that thenceforth their subsidies would be reduced. The chiefs strongly remonstrated, but without effect, and they then formed a confederacy of rebellion. The Ghilzai chiefs were the first to act. Quitting Cabul, they occupied the passes between the capital and Jellalabad, and entirely intercepted the communications with India by the Khyber route.

Macnaghten did not take alarm at this significant demonstration, regarding the outbreak merely as 'provoking,' and writing to Rawlinson that 'the rascals would be well trounced for their pains.' Yet warnings of gathering danger were rife, which but for his mood of optimism should have struck home to his apprehension. Pottinger had come down from the Kohistan, where he was acting as political officer, bent on impressing on him that a general rising of that region was certain unless strong measures of prevention were resorted to. For some time before the actual outbreak of the Ghilzais, the Afghan hatred to our people had been showing itself with exceptional openness and bitterness. Europeans and camp followers had been murdered, but the sinister evidences of growing danger had been regarded merely as ebullitions of private rancour. Akbar Khan, Dost Mahomed's son, had moved forward from Khooloom into the Bamian country, and there was little doubt that he was fomenting the disaffection of the Ghilzai chiefs, with some of whom this indomitable man, who in his intense hatred of the English intruders had resolutely rejected all offers of accommodation, and preferred the life of a homeless exile to the forfeiture of his independence, was closely connected by marriage.

The time was approaching when Sale's brigade was to quit Cabul on its return journey to India. Macnaghten seems to have originally intended to accompany this force, for he wrote that he 'hoped to settle the hash of the Ghilzais on the way down, if not before.' The rising, however, spread so widely and so rapidly that immediate action was judged necessary, and on October 9th Colonel Monteath marched towards the passes with his own regiment, the 35th Native Infantry, some artillery and cavalry details, and a detachment of Broadfoot's sappers.

How able, resolute, and high-souled a man was George Broadfoot, the course of this narrative will later disclose. He was one of three gallant brothers, all of whom died sword in hand. The corps of sappers which he commanded was a remarkable body—a strange medley of Hindustanees, Goorkhas, and Afghan tribesmen of divers regions. Many were desperate and intractable characters, but Broadfoot, with mingled strength and kindness, moulded his heterogeneous recruits into skilful, obedient and disciplined soldiers. Broadfoot's description of his endeavours to learn something of the nature of the duties expected of him in the expedition for which he had been detailed, and to obtain such equipment as those duties might require, throws a melancholy light on the deteriorated state of affairs among our people at this period, and on the relations between the military and civilian authorities.

Broadfoot went for information, in the first instance, to Colonel Monteath, who could give him no orders, having received none himself. Monteath declined to apply for details as to the expedition, as he knew 'these people' (the authorities) too well; he was quite aware of the danger of going on service in the dark, but explained that it was not the custom of the military authorities at Cabul to consult or even instruct the commanders of expeditions. Broadfoot then went to the General. Cotton's successor in the chief military command in Afghanistan was poor General Elphinstone, a most gallant soldier, but with no experience of Indian warfare, and utterly ignorant of the Afghans and of Afghanistan. Wrecked in body and impaired in mind by physical ailments and infirmities, he had lost all faculty of energy, and such mind as remained to him was swayed by the opinion of the person with whom he had last spoken. The poor gentleman was so exhausted by the exertion of getting out of bed, and being helped into his visiting-room, that it was not for half-an-hour, and after several ineffectual efforts, that he could attend to business. He knew nothing of the nature of the service on which Monteath was ordered, could give Broadfoot no orders, and was unwilling to refer to the Envoy on a matter which should have been left to him to arrange. He complained bitterly of the way in which he was reduced to a cypher—'degraded from a general to the "Lord-Lieutenant's head constable."' Broad-

foot went from the General to the Envoy, who 'was pee-
vish,' and denounced the General as fidgety. He declared
the enemy to be contemptible, and that as for Broadfoot
and his sappers, twenty men with pickaxes were enough;
all they were wanted for was to pick stones from under the
gun wheels. When Broadfoot represented the inconven-
ience with which imperfect information as to the objects
of the expedition was fraught, Macnaghten lost his temper,
and told Broadfoot that, if he thought Monteath's movement likely to bring on an attack, 'he need not go, he was
not wanted'; whereupon Broadfoot declined to listen to
such language, and made his bow. Returning to the General, whom he found 'lost and perplexed,' he was told to
follow his own judgment as to what quantity of tools he
should take. The Adjutant-General came in, and 'this officer, after abusing the Envoy, spoke to the General with an
imperiousness and disrespect, and to me, a stranger, with
an insolence it was painful to see the influence of on the
General. His advice to his chief was to have nothing to say
to Macnaghten, to me, or to the sappers, saying Monteath
had men enough, and needed neither sappers nor tools.' At
parting the poor old man said to Broadfoot: 'If you go out,
for God's sake clear the passes quickly, that I may get away;
for if anything were to turn up, I am unfit for it, done up in
body and mind.' This was the man whom Lord Auckland
had appointed to the most responsible and arduous command at his disposal, and this not in ignorance of General
Elphinstone's disqualifications for active service, but in the
fullest knowledge of them!

Monteath's camp at Bootkhak, the first halting-place on
the Jellalabad road, was sharply attacked on the night of
the 9th, and the assailants, many of whom were the armed
retainers of chiefs living in Cabul sent out specially to take
part in the attack, although unsuccessful, inflicted on Mont-

eath considerable loss. Next day Sale, with H.M.'s 13th, joined Monteath, and on the 13th he forced the long and dangerous ravine of the Khoord Cabul with sharp fighting, but no very serious loss, although Sale himself was wounded, and had to relinquish the active command to Colonel Dennie. Monteath encamped in the valley beyond the pass, and Sale, with the 13th, returned without opposition to Bootkhak, there to await reinforcements and transports. In his isolated position Monteath remained unmolested until the night of the 17th, when he repulsed a Ghilzai attack made in considerable strength, and aided by the treachery of 'friendly' Afghans who had been admitted into his camp; but he had many casualties, and lost a number of camels. On the 20th Sale, reinforced by troops returned from the Zurmut expedition, moved forward on Monteath, and on the 22d pushed on to the Tezeen valley, meeting with no opposition either on the steep summit of the Huft Kotul or in the deep narrow ravine opening into the valley. The Ghilzais were in force around the mouth of the defile, but a few cannon-shots broke them up. The advance guard pursued with over-rashness; the Ghilzais rallied, in the skirmish which ensued an officer and several men were killed, and the retirement of our people unfortunately degenerated into precipitate flight, with the Ghilzais in hot pursuit. The 13th, to which the fugitive detachment mainly belonged, now consisted mainly of young soldiers, whose constancy was impaired by this untoward occurrence.

Macnaghten had furnished Sale with a force which, in good heart and vigorously commanded, was strong enough to have effected great things. The Ghilzai chief of Tezeen possessed a strong fort full of supplies, which Dennie was about to attack, when the wily Afghan sent to Major Macgregor, the political officer accompanying Sale, a tender of submission. Macgregor fell into the snare, desired Sale to countermand the attack, and entered into negotiations. In doing so he committed a fatal error, and he exceeded his instructions in the concessions which he made. Macnaghten, it was true, had left matters greatly to Macgregor's discretion; and if 'the rebels were very humble,' the Envoy was not disposed to be too hard upon them. But one of his firm stipulations was that the defences of Khoda Buxsh's fort must be demolished, and that Gool Mahomed Khan 'should have nothing but war.' Both injunctions were disregarded by Macgregor, who, with unimportant exceptions, surrendered all along the line. The Ghilzais claimed and obtained the restoration of their original subsidies; a sum was handed to them to enable them to raise the tribes in order to keep clear the passes; Khoda Buxsh held his fort, and sold the supplies it contained to Sale's commissary at a fine price. Every item of the arrangement was dead in favour of the Ghilzais, and contributory to their devices. Sale, continuing his march, would be separated further and further from the now diminished force in Cabul, and by the feigned submission the chiefs had made they had escaped the permanent establishment of a strong detachment in their midst at Tezeen.

Macnaghten, discontented though he was with the sweeping concessions which Macgregor had granted to the Ghilzais, put the best face he could on the completed transaction, and allowed himself to believe that a stable settlement had been effected. On the 26th Sale continued his march, having made up his baggage animals at the expense of the 37th Native Infantry, which, with half of the sappers and three guns of the mountain train, he sent back to Kubbar-i-Jubbar, there to halt in a dangerously helpless situation until transport should be sent down from Cabul. His march as far as Kutti Sung was unmolested. Mistrusting the good faith of his new-made allies, he shunned the usual

route through the Purwan Durrah by taking the mountain road to the south of that defile, and thus reached the
Jugdulluk valley with little opposition, baulking the dispositions of the Ghilzais, who, expecting him to traverse the
Purwan Durrah, were massed about the southern end of
the defile, ready to fall on the column when committed to
the tortuous gorge.

From the Jugdulluk camping ground there is a steep
and winding ascent of three miles, commanded until near
the summit by heights on either side. Sale's main body
had attained the crest with trivial loss, having detached
parties by the way to ascend to suitable flanking positions, and hold those until the long train of slow-moving
baggage should have passed, when they were to fall in
and come on with the rear-guard. The dispositions would
have been successful but that on reaching the crest the
main body, instead of halting there for the rear to close
up, hurried down the reverse slope, leaving baggage, detachments, and rear-guard to endure the attacks which
the Ghilzais promptly delivered, pressing fiercely on the
rear, and firing down from either side on the confused
mass in the trough below. The flanking detachments had
relinquished their posts in panic, and hurried forward in
confusion to get out of the pass. The rear-guard was in
disorder, when Broadfoot, with a few officers and some of
his sappers, valiantly checked the onslaught, but the crest
was not crossed until upwards of 120 men had fallen, the
wounded among whom had to be abandoned with the
dead. On October 30th Sale's force reached Gundamuk
without further molestation, and halted there temporarily to await orders. During the halt melancholy rumours
filtered down the passes from the capital, and later came
confirmation of the evil tidings from the Envoy, and orders from Elphinstone directing the immediate return of

the brigade to Cabul, if the safety of its sick and wounded could be assured. Sale called a council of war, which pronounced, although not unanimously, against a return to Cabul; and it was resolved instead to march on to Jellalabad, which was regarded as an eligible point d'appui on which a relieving force might move up and a retiring force might move down. Accordingly on November 11th the brigade quitted Gundamuk, and hurried down rather precipitately, and with some fighting by the way, to Jellalabad, which was occupied on the 14th.

Some members of the Gundamuk council of war, foremost among whom was Broadfoot, argued vigorously in favour of the return march to Cabul. Havelock, who was with Sale as a staff-officer, strongly urged the further retreat into Jellalabad. Others, again, advocated the middle course of continuing to hold Gundamuk. It may be said that a daring general would have fought his way back to Cabul, that a prudent general would have remained at Gundamuk, and that the occupation of Jellalabad was the expedient of a weak general. That a well-led march on Cabul was feasible, although it might have been difficult and bloody, cannot be questioned, and the advent of such men as Broadfoot and Havelock would have done much toward rekindling confidence and stimulating the restoration of soldierly virtue, alike in the military authorities and in the rank and file of the Cabul force. At Gundamuk, again, the brigade, well able to maintain its position there, would have made its influence felt all through the Ghilzai country and as far as Cabul. The evacuation of that capital decided on, it would have been in a position to give the hand to the retiring army, and so to avert at least the worst disasters of the retreat. The retirement on Jellalabad, in the terse language of Durand, 'served no conceivable purpose except to betray weakness, and still further to encourage revolt.'

While Sale was struggling through the passes on his way to Gundamuk, our people at Cabul were enjoying unwonted quietude. Casual entries in Lady Sale's journal, during the later days of October, afford clear evidence how utterly unconscious were they of the close gathering of the storm that so soon was to break upon them. Her husband had written to her from Tezeen that his wound was fast healing, and that the chiefs were extremely polite. She complains of the interruption of the mails owing to the Ghilzai outbreak, but comforts herself with the anticipation of their arrival in a day or two. She was to leave Cabul for India in a few days, along with the Macnaghtens and General Elphinstone, and her diary expresses an undernote of regret at having to leave the snug house in the cantonments which Sale had built on his own plan, the excellent kitchen garden in which her warrior husband, in the intervals of his soldiering duties, grew fine crops of peas, potatoes, cauliflowers and artichokes, and the parterres of flowers which she herself cultivated, and which were the admiration of the Afghan gentlemen who came to pay their morning calls.

The defencelessness of the position at Cabul had long engaged the solicitude of men who were no alarmists. Engineer officer after engineer officer had unavailingly and a half from the cantonments, with the Cabul river intervening. With Shelton's troops and those in the cantonments General Elphinstone had at his disposition, apart from the Shah's contingent, four infantry regiments, two batteries of artillery, three companies of sappers, a regiment of cavalry, and some irregular horse—a force fully equipped and in good order. In the Balla Hissar Shah Soojah had a considerable, if rather mixed, body of military and several guns.

The rising of the 2d November may not have been the result of a fully organised plan. There are indications that it was premature, and that the revolt in force would have been postponed until after the expected departure of the Envoy and the General with all the troops except Shelton's brigade, but for an irrepressible burst of personal rancour against Burnes. Durand holds, however, that the malcontents acted on the belief that to kill Burnes and sack the Treasury was to inaugurate the insurrection with an imposing success. Be this as it may, a truculent mob early in the morning of November 2nd assailed Burnes' house. He at first regarded the outbreak as a casual riot, and wrote to Macnaghten to that effect. Having harangued the throng without effect, he and his brother, along with William Broadfoot his secretary, prepared for defence. Broadfoot was soon killed, and a little later Burnes and his brother were hacked to pieces in the garden behind the house. The Treasury was sacked; the sepoys who had guarded it and Burnes' house were massacred, and both buildings were fired; the armed mob swelled in numbers, and soon the whole city was in a roar of tumult.

Prompt and vigorous military action would no doubt have crushed the insurrection, at least for the time. But the indifference, vacillation and delay of the British authorities greatly encouraged its rapid development. Macnaghten at first 'did not think much of it.' Shelton was ordered into the Balla Hissar, countermanded, a second time ordered, and again instructed to halt for orders. At last the Envoy himself despatched him, with the loose order to act on his own judgment in communication with the Shah. Shelton marched into the Balla Hissar with part of his force, and the rest of it was moved into the cantonments. When the Brigadier went to the Shah, that potentate demanded to know who sent him, and what he had come for. But the Shah, to do him justice, had himself taken action. Informed that Burnes was attacked and the city in revolt, he had ordered Campbell's regiment of his own levies and a couple of guns to march to his assistance. Campbell reck-lessly attempted to push his way through the heart of the city, instead of reaching Burnes' house by a circuitous but opener route, and after some sharp street fighting in which he lost heavily, he was driven back, unable to penetrate to the scene of plunder and butchery. Shelton remained inactive in the Balla Hissar until Campbell was reported beaten and retreating, when he took some feeble measures to cover the retreat of the fugitives, who, however, abandoned their guns outside the fortress. The day was allowed to pass without anything further being done, except the despatch of an urgent recall to Major Griffiths, whom Sale had left at Kubbar-i-Jubbar, and that good soldier, having fought every step of the way through the passes, brought in his detachment in unbroken order and without loss of baggage, notwithstanding his weakness in transport. Shelton, reinforced in the Balla Hissar, maintained an intermittent and ineffectual fire on the city. Urgent orders were despatched to Sale, recalling him and his brigade—orders with which, as has been mentioned, Sale did not comply—and also to Nott, at Candahar, begging him to send a brigade to Cabul. In compliance with this requisition, Maclaren's brigade immediately started from Candahar, but soon returned owing to the inclemency of the weather.

Captain Mackenzie was in charge of a fort containing the Shah's commissariat stores; this fort was on the outskirts of a suburb of Cabul, and was fiercely attacked on the 2d. For two days Mackenzie maintained his post with unwearying constancy. His garrison was short of water and of ammunition, and the fort was crowded with women and children, but he held on resolutely until the night of the 3d. No assistance was sent, no notice, indeed, of any kind was taken of him; his garrison was discouraged by heavy loss, and by the mines which the enemy were pushing forward. At length, when the gate of the fort had been fired, and his wounded were dying for lack of medical aid, he evacuated the fort, and fought his way gallantly into cantonments, bringing in his wounded and the women and children. With this solitary exception the Afghans had nowhere encountered resistance, and the strange passiveness of our people encouraged them to act with vigour. From the enclosed space of the Shah Bagh, and the adjacent forts of Mahmood Khan and Mahomed Shereef, they were threatening the Commissariat fort, hindering access to it, and besetting the south-western flank of the cantonments. A young officer commanded the hundred sepoys garrisoning the Commissariat fort; he reported himself in danger of being cut off, and Elphinstone gave orders that he and his garrison should be brought off, and the fort and its contents abandoned. Several efforts to accomplish the withdrawal were thwarted by the Afghan flanking fire, with the loss of several officers and many men. The commissary officer urged on the General the disastrous consequences which the abandonment of the fort would entail, containing as it did all the stores, adding that in cantonments there were only two days' supplies, without prospect of procuring any more. Orders were then sent to Warren to hold out to the last extremity; which instructions he denied having received. Early in the morning of the 5th troops were preparing to attack the Afghan fort and reinforce the Commissariat fort, when Warren and his garrison reached the cantonments. The gate of the Commissariat fort had been fired, but the enemy had not effected an entrance, yet Warren and his people had evacuated the fort through a hole cut in its wall. Thus, with scarcely a struggle to save it, was this vital fort allowed to fall into the enemy's hands, and thenceforward our unfortunate people were to be reduced to precarious and scanty sources for their food.

From the 5th to the 9th November there was a good deal of desultory fighting, in the course of which, after one failure, Mahomed Shereef's fort was stormed by a detachment of our people, under the command of Major Griffiths; but this success had little influence on the threatening attitude maintained by the Afghans. On the 9th, owing to the mental and physical weakness of poor General Elphinstone, Brigadier Shelton was summoned into cantonments from the Balla Hissar, bringing with him part of the garrison with which he had been holding the latter post. The hopes entertained that Shelton would display vigour, and restore the confidence of the troops, were not realised. He from the first had no belief in the ability of the occupants of the cantonment to maintain their position, and he never ceased to urge prompt retreat on Jellalabad. From the purely military point of view he was probably right; the Duke of Wellington shared his opinion when he said in the House of Lords: 'After the first few days, particularly after the negotiations at Cabul had commenced, it became hopeless for General Elphinstone to maintain his position.' Shelton's situation was unquestionably a very uncomfortable one, for Elphinstone, broken as he was, yet allowed his second in command no freedom of action, and was testily pertinacious of his prerogative of command. If in Shelton, who after his manner was a strong man, there had been combined with his resolution some tact and temper, he might have exercised a beneficial influence. As it was he became sullen and despondent, and retired behind an 'uncommunicative and disheartening reserve.' Brave as he was, he seems to have lacked the inspiration which alone could reinvigorate the drooping spirit of the troops. In a word, though he probably was, in army language, a 'good duty soldier,' he certainly was nothing more. And something more was needed then.

Action on Shelton's part became necessary the day after he came into cantonments. The Afghans occupied all the forts on the plain between the Seah Sung heights and the cantonments, and from the nearest of them, the Rikabashee fort, poured in a heavy fire at close range, which the return artillery fire could not quell. On Macnaghten's urgent requisition the General ordered out a strong force, under Shelton, to storm the obnoxious fort. Captain Bellew missed the gate, and blew open merely a narrow wicket, but the storming party obeyed the signal to advance. Through a heavy fire the leaders reached the wicket, and forced their way in, followed by a few soldiers. The garrison of the fort hastily evacuated it, and all seemed well, when a sudden stampede ensued—the handful which, led by Colonel Mackrell of the 44th and Lieutenant Bird of the Shah's force, had already entered the fort, remaining inside it. The runaway troops were rallied with difficulty by Shelton and the subordinate officers, but a call for volunteers from the European regiment was responded to but by one solitary Scottish private. After a second advance, and a second retreat—a retreat made notwithstanding strong artillery and musketry support—Shelton's efforts brought his people forward yet again, and this time the fort was occupied in force. Of those who had previously entered it but two survivors were found. The Afghans, re-entering the fort, had hacked Mackrell to pieces and slaughtered the men who tried to escape by the wicket. Lieutenant Bird and a sepoy, from a stable the door of which they had barricaded with logs of wood, had fended off their assailants by a steady and deadly fire, and when they were rescued by the entrance of the troops they had to clamber out over a pile of thirty dead Afghans whom the bullets of the two men had struck down.

It had come to our people in those gloomy days, to

regard as a 'triumph' a combat in which they were not actually worsted; and even of such dubious successes the last occurred on November 13, when the Afghans, after having pressed our infantry down the slopes of the Behmaroo ridge, were driven back by artillery fire, and forced by a cavalry charge to retreat further, leaving behind them a couple of guns from which they had been sending missiles into the cantonments. One of those guns was brought in without difficulty, but the other the Afghans covered with their jezail fire. The Envoy had sent a message of entreaty that 'the triumph of the day' should be completed by its capture. Major Scott of the 44th made appeal on appeal, ineffectually, to the soldierly feelings of his men, and while they would not move the sepoys could not be induced to advance. At length Eyre spiked the piece as a precautionary measure, and finally some men of the Shah's infantry succeeded in bringing in the prize. The return march of the troops into cantonments in the dark, was rendered disorderly by the close pressure of the Afghans, who, firing incessantly, pursued the broken soldiery up to the entrance gate.

On the depressed garrison of the Cabul cantonments tidings of disaster further afield had been pouring in apace. Soon after the outbreak of the rising, it was known that Lieutenant Maule, commanding the Kohistanee regiment at Kurdurrah, had been cut to pieces, with his adjutant and sergeant-major, by the men of his own corps; and on November 6th intelligence had come in that the Goorkha regiment stationed at Charikar in the Kohistan, where Major Pottinger was Resident, was in dangerous case, and that Codrington, its commandant, and some of his officers had already fallen. And now, on the 15th, there rode wearily into cantonments two wounded men, who believed themselves the only British survivors of the Charikar force. Pottinger was wounded in the leg, Haughton, the adjutant of the Goorkha corps, had lost his right hand, and his head hung forward on his breast, half severed from his body by a great tulwar slash. Of the miserable story which it fell to Pottinger to tell only the briefest summary can be given. His residence was at Lughmanee, a few miles from the Charikar cantonments, when early in the month a number of chiefs of the Kohistan and the Nijrao country assembled to discuss with him the terms on which they would reopen the communications with Cabul. Those chiefs proved treacherous, slew Rattray, Pottinger's assistant, and besieged Pottinger in Lughmanee. Finding his position untenable, he withdrew to Charikar under cover of night. On the morning of the 5th the Afghans assailed the cantonments. Pottinger was wounded, Codrington was killed, and the Goorkhas were driven into the barracks. Haughton, who succeeded to the command of the regiment, made sortie on sortie, but was finally driven in, and the enemy renewed their assaults in augmented strength. Thenceforward the position was all but hopeless. On the 10th the last scant remains of water was distributed. Efforts to procure water by sorties on the nights of the 11th and 12th were not successful, and the corps fell into disorganisation because of losses, hardships, exhaustion, hunger and thirst. Pottinger and Haughton agreed that there was no prospect of saving even a remnant of the regiment unless by a retreat to Cabul, which, however, was clearly possible only in the case of the stronger men, unencumbered with women and children, of whom, unfortunately, there was a great number in the garrison. On the afternoon of the 13th Haughton was cut down by a treacherous native officer of the artillery, who then rushed out of the gate, followed by all the gunners and most of the Mahommedans of the garrison. In the midst of the chaos of disorganisation, Dr Grant amputated Haughton's hand, dressed his other wounds, and then spiked all the guns. When it was dark, the garrison moved out, Pottinger leading the advance, Dr Grant the main body, and Ensign Rose the rear-guard. From the beginning of the march, discipline was all but entirely in abeyance; on reaching the first stream, the last remains of control were lost, and the force was rapidly disintegrating. Pottinger and Haughton, the latter only just able to keep the saddle, pushed on toward Cabul, rested in a ravine during the day, evaded the partisan detachment sent out from Cabul to intercept them, rode through sleeping Cabul in the small hours of the morning, and after being pursued and fired upon in the outskirts of the city, finally attained the cantonments. It was afterwards learned that a portion of the regiment had struggled on to within twenty miles from Cabul, gallantly headed by young Rose and Dr Grant. Then the remnant was destroyed. Rose was killed, after despatching four Afghans with his own hand. Dr Grant, escaping the massacre, held on until within three miles of the cantonments, when he too was killed.

Macnaghten was naturally much depressed by the news communicated by Pottinger, and realised that the Afghan masses already encompassing the position on the Cabul plain would certainly be increased by bands from the Kohistan and Nijrao, flushed already with their Charikar success. He sided strongly with the large party among the officers who were advocating the measure of abandoning the cantonments altogether, and moving the force now quartered there to the safer and more commanding position in the Balla Hissar. The military chiefs opposed the project, and propounded a variety of objections to it, none of which were without weight, yet all of which might have been overcome by energy and proper dispositions. Shelton, however, was opposed to the scheme, since if carried out it would avert or postpone the accomplishment of his policy of retreat on Jellalabad; Elphinstone was against it in the inertia of debility, and the project gradually came to be regarded as abandoned. Another project, that of driving the Afghans from Mahmood Khan's fort, commanding the direct road between the cantonments and the Balla Hissar, and of occupying it with a British force, was so far advanced that the time for the attempt was fixed, and the storming party actually warned, when some petty objection intervened and the enterprise was abandoned, never to be revived.

The rising was not three days old when already Elphinstone had lost heart. On the 5th he had written to Macnaghten suggesting that the latter should 'consider what chance there is of making terms,' and since then he had been repeatedly pressing on the Envoy the 'hopelessness of further resistance.' Macnaghten, vacillating as he was, yet had more pith in his nature than was left in the debilitated old general. He wrote to Elphinstone on the 18th recommending, not very strenuously, the policy of holding out where they were as long as possible, and indeed throughout the winter, if subsistence could be obtained. He pointed out that in the cantonments, which he believed to be impregnable, there were at least the essentials of wood and water. Arguing that a retreat on Jellalabad must be most disastrous, and was to be avoided except in the last extremity, he nevertheless ended somewhat inconsistently by leaving to the military authorities, if in eight or ten days there should appear no prospect of an improvement of the situation, the decision whether it would be wiser to attempt a retreat or to withdraw from the cantonments into the Balla Hissar.

Far from improving, the situation was speedily to become all but hopeless. The village of Behmaroo, built on the north-eastern slope of the ridge of the same name bounding the plain on the north-west, lay about half a mile due north of the cantonments, part of which some of the houses on the upper slope commanded. From this village, after the loss of the Commissariat fort, our people had been drawing supplies. On the morning of the 22d the Afghans were seen moving in force from Cabul toward Behmaroo, obviously with intent to occupy the village, and so deprive the occupants of the cantonments of the resource it had been affording them. A detachment under Major Swayne, sent out to forestall this occupation, found Behmaroo already in the possession of a body of Kohistanees, who had so blocked the approaches that Swayne did not consider himself justified in attempting the fulfilment of his orders to storm the place; and he contented himself with maintaining all day an ineffectual musketry fire on it. A diversion in his favour by a gun supported by cavalry had no result save that of casualties to the gunners and troopers; reinforcements brought out by Shelton effected nothing, and in the evening the troops were recalled. On this ill-fated day Akbar Khan, Dost Mahomed's fierce and implacable son, arrived in Cabul, and the evil influence on the British fortunes which he exerted immediately made itself felt, for the events of the following day were to bring about a crisis in the fate of our ill-starred people.

Recognising the mischief wrought by the hostile occupation of our only source of supplies, the Envoy strongly urged the immediate despatch of a strong force to occupy the Behmaroo ridge, and dislodge from the village its Kohistanee garrison. Shelton opposed the measure, urging the dispirited state of the troops, their fatigue from constant defensive duty, and their weakened physique because of poor and scanty rations. He was overruled, and before daybreak of the 23d a force under his command, consisting of five companies of the 44th, twelve companies of native infantry, some cavalry, and one horse-artillery gun, was in position on the north-eastern extremity of the ridge overhanging the village. The gun opened fire on the village with grape, and after a short resistance the greater part of its garrison quitted it. The storming party intrusted to Major Swayne did not, however, act, and was withdrawn. Leaving a detachment on the knoll above the village, Shelton moved his force along the upland to a position near the gorge intersecting the ridge, forming his infantry into two squares, with the cavalry in rear. The further hill beyond the gorge was crowded with hostile Afghans from Cabul, and the long-range fire of their jezails across the dividing depression, carried execution into the squares which Shelton had inexplicably formed as if to furnish his foes with a target which they could not miss. The muskets of his men could not retaliate, and the skirmishers he threw forward to the brow of his hill could not endure the Afghan fire. Shelton's single gun maintained a hot and telling fire on the Afghan masses on the opposite hill, and baulked an attempt against his right flank made by the Afghan cavalry swarming in the outer plain; but when its vent became too hot for the gunners to serve it, the dullest comprehension became alive to the folly of sending a single gun into the field.

Shelton's men, falling fast though they were, and faint with fatigue and thirst, yet had endured for hours a fusillade to which they could not reply, when a body of Afghan fanatics suddenly sprang up out of the gorge, swept back with their fire the few skirmishers who had been still holding the brow of the hill, and planted their flag within thirty yards of the front of the nearer of the squares. Shelton offered a large reward to the man who should bring it in, but there was no response. In a passion of soldierly wrath, the veteran commanded a bayonet charge; not a man sprang forward at the summons which British soldiers are wont to welcome with cheers. The cowed infantry remained supine, when their officers darted forward and threw stones into the faces of the enemy; the troopers heard but obeyed not that trumpet-call to 'Charge!' which so rarely fails to thrill the cavalryman with the rapture of the fray. The gunners only, men of that noble force the Company's Horse-Artillery, quitted themselves valiantly. They stood to their piece to the bitter end. Two of them were killed beside it, another was severely wounded, a fourth, refusing to run, took refuge under the gun, and miraculously escaped death. But the gallant example of the artillerymen in their front did not hearten the infantrymen of the leading square. The panic spread among them, and they broke and fled. Fortunately they were not pursued. The rear square stood fast, and the officers by great exertion succeeded in rallying the fugitives under the cover it afforded. The news that a principal chief, Abdoolah Khan, had been severely wounded in the plain gave pause to the offensive vigour of the Afghans, and the assailants fell back, abandoning the gun, but carrying off the limber and gun-team. Our people reoccupied the position, the gun recommenced its fire, and if the cavalry and infantry could have been persuaded to take the offensive the battle might have been retrieved. But they remained passive. The reinforced Afghans renewed their long-range fire with terrible effect; most of the gunners had fallen, and the Brigadier, recognising the growing unsteadiness of his command and the imminent danger of capture to which the solitary gun was again exposed, ordered a retirement on the detachment left near Behmaroo and the limbering up of the gun, to which a second limber had been sent out from the cantonments. The movement was scarcely begun when a rush of fanatic Afghans completely broke the square, and all order and discipline then disappeared. A regular rout set in down the hill toward cantonments, the fugitives disregarding the efforts of the officers to rally them, and the enemy in full pursuit, the Afghan cavalry making ghastly slaughter among the panic-stricken runaways. The detachment near Behmaroo attempted to fall back in orderly fashion, but the reinforced garrison of the village swept out upon it, surrounded it, broke it up, and threw it into utter rout with the loss of a large proportion of its strength, one whole company being all but annihilated. It seemed as if pursued and pursuers would enter the cantonments together so closely were they commingled; but the fire from the ramparts and an opportune charge of horse arrested the pursuit. Yet Eyre reckons as the chief reason why all the British force that had gone out to battle was not destroyed, the fact that a leading Afghan chief forced his men to spare the fugitives, and ultimately halted and withdrew his people when the opportunity for wholesale slaughter lay open to them. Most of the wounded were left on the field, where they were miserably cut to pieces; and the gun, which had been overturned in the attempt of the drivers to gallop down the face of the hill, finally passed into the possession of the Afghans. Shelton's dispositions as a commander could not well have been worse; his bearing as a soldier, although undaunted, imparted to his hapless troops nothing of inspiration. The obstinacy with which he held the hill after the impossibility of even partial success must have been patent to him, was universally condemned. It need scarcely be added that his loss was very severe.

No more fighting was possible. What, then, was to be done? Elphinstone and Shelton were at one in opposing removal into the Balla Hissar. Macnaghten, to whom Shah Soojah had communicated his urgent recommendation of that measure as the only expedient which could secure the safety of the British troops, fell in with the views of the military authorities. There came to him a letter from Osman Khan, the chief who had called off his adherents on

BALAR HISSAR CABUL

the previous day from pursuing the fugitives fleeing into cantonments. Osman wrote that, if his troops had followed up their successes, the loss of the cantonments and the destruction of the British force were inevitable; but, he continued, that it was not the wish of the chiefs to proceed to such extremities, their sole desire being that our people should quietly evacuate the country, leaving the Afghan sirdars to govern it according to their own customs, and with a king of their own choosing. In communicating this letter to General Elphinstone, Sir William asked for the latter's opinion on the military possibility, or the reverse, of the retention of the British position in Afghanistan. Elphinstone, in reply, enumerated sundry reasons which led him to the conclusion which he stated, that 'it is not feasible any longer to maintain our position in this country, and that you ought to avail yourself of the offer to negotiate which has been made to you.'

CHAPTER 6

The Road to Ruin

As the result of the military disaster of November 23d, and of the representations of the General, recorded in the last chapter, Macnaghten, with whatever reluctance, permitted himself to entertain proposals for an arrangement made by the Afghan leaders. From the beginning of the outbreak, while urging on the military authorities to exert themselves in putting down the revolt, he had been engaged in tortuous and dangerous intrigues, with the object of sowing discord among the Afghan chiefs, and thus weakening the league of hostility against Shah Soojah and his British supporters. In the conduct of these intrigues he used the services of Mohun Lal, who had been one of Burnes' assistants, and who, having escaped the fate of his chief, had found refuge in the city residence of a Kuzzilbash chief. Mohun Lal was a fitting agent for the sort of work prescribed to him, and he burrowed and suborned with assiduity, and not altogether without success. But it is unhappily true that he was commissioned to carry out a darker enterprise, the removal by assassination of certain of the more virulently hostile among the Afghan leaders. The incident is the blackest of the many discreditable transactions which chequer the inner political history of this melancholy chapter of our annals. It is unfortunately certain that Lieutenant John Conolly, Macnaghten's kinsman and his confidential representative with Shah Soojah, authorised Mohun Lal, in writing, to compass the taking off of prominent Afghan leaders. In a letter to Mohun Lal, of 5th November, Conolly wrote: 'I promise 10,000 rupees for the head of each rebel chief.' Again, on the 11th, he wrote: 'There is a man called Hadji Ali, who might be induced by a bribe to try and bring in the heads of one or two of the Mufsids. Endeavour to let him know that 10,000 rupees will be given for each head, or even 15,000 rupees.' Two chiefs certainly did die under suspicious circumstances, and in each case the blood–money was claimed. It was refused by Mohun Lal on the plea that the stipulation that the heads of the dead Afghans should be brought in was not fulfilled.

Whether Macnaghten inspired those nefarious machinations, whether indeed he was actively aware of them, are questions which, in the absence of conclusive evidence, may judiciously be left unanswered. There is extant a letter from him to Mohun Lal, written December 1st, which has the following passage: 'I am sorry to find from your letter of last night that you should have supposed it was ever my object to encourage assassination. The rebels are very wicked men, but we must not take unlawful means to destroy them.' And later he is reported to have informed an Afghan deputation that, 'as a British functionary, nothing would induce him to pay a price for blood.' Durand holds that it was the belief on the part of the Afghan chiefs that the British Envoy had set a price on their heads which destroyed all confidence in Macnaghten's good faith, and which was Akbar Khan's chief incentive to his murder.

The terms proffered on November 25th by an Afghan deputation were so humiliating that Macnaghten peremptorily rejected them; and the threat of immediate hostilities unless our people promptly surrendered their arms and withdrew was not carried out. A period of inaction strangely ensued, which on the Afghan side was a treacherous lull, but which Macnaghten, hoping against hope that some turn in our favour might yet occur, regarded with complacency. The chiefs, aware that winter was approaching with added hardship to the forlorn garrison, temporarily desisted from urging negotiations. But the British military authorities, with troops living from hand to mouth on precarious half rations, and with transport cattle dying fast of starvation, kept urging the Envoy to activity in making terms, if absolute starvation was to be averted. Futile projects were discussed between Envoy and General, only to be put aside. As the dreary days of inaction and depletion passed, the deterioration of military spirit among our people manifested itself more and more plainly. British soldiers stolidly watched the Afghans destroying our bridge across the Cabul river, within a quarter of a mile from cantonments. Scared by the threat of an assault, which, in the scornful words of brave Lady Sale, a child with a stick might have repulsed, the garrison of the Mahomed Shereef fort abandoned it in a panic, the white soldiers of the 44th showing the example of pusillanimity to the sepoys whom their cowardice demoralised. Next day the detachment of the 44th which had guarded an exposed position had to be withdrawn, ceding the post of honour to the stauncher sepoys. The camp followers were living on carrion; the commissaries reported but four days' provisions in store, and their inability to procure any more supplies. At length on December 8th the four senior military officers informed the Envoy that it was imperatively necessary he should negotiate a retreat, on the best terms he could obtain.

Macnaghten had to bring himself to recognise that the alternatives were negotiation or starvation, and on the 11th December, with a draft treaty in his hand, he met the principal Afghan chiefs on the river side between the cantonments and the city. After the introductory palavers, Macnaghten read the proposed treaty, whose purport was as follows: that the British should evacuate Afghanistan forthwith unmolested, furnished with supplies and accompanied by hostages, on their march to India; that the Dost, his family, and other Afghan political exiles, should be allowed to return to their country; that Shah Soojah should have the option of remaining at Cabul or going down to India; that amnesty should be accorded to all adherents of Shah Soojah and his British allies; that all prisoners should be released; and that perpetual friendship and mutual good offices should thenceforth endure between the British and the Afghans.

Akbar Khan made demur to some of the provisions, but was overruled, and the main stipulations of the treaty were agreed to by the chiefs. The conference broke up with the understanding that the British troops should evacuate cantonments within three days, and that meanwhile provisions should be sent in for their use. The treaty was simply a virtual capitulation all along the line; but the inherent falseness of our position, the incapacity of the military chiefs, and the debased spirit of the troops, consequent partly on low rations but mainly because of the utter absence of competent and vigorous leadership such as a Broadfoot or a Havelock would have supplied, enforced on the reluctant Envoy conditions humiliating beyond previous parallel in the history of our nation.

From the outset the Afghan chiefs defaulted from their promise of sending in supplies, but some grain was brought into cantonments by the troops, whose evacuation of the Balla Hissar on the 13th was effected under humiliating circumstances. The Afghans demanded the surrender of the forts in British occupation in the vicinity of the cantonments. The requisition was complied with, and the Magazine fort furnished the enemy with both arms and ammunition.

The three stipulated days passed away, and still the British force remained motionless in the cantonments. Macnaghten was bent on procrastination, and circumstances seemed to favour a policy which to all but himself was inexplicable. By the treaty, Shah Soojah was in effect committed to withdraw to India, but soon after its acceptance the chiefs had invited him to remain in Cabul as king, on the stipulation that he should give his daughters in marriage to leaders of the malcontents. After considerable deliberation, the Shah had consented to remain on the condition named, but a few days later he withdrew his acceptance. His vacillation increased the suspicions of the chiefs, and they demanded the immediate evacuation of the cantonments, refusing to furnish provisions until that was done. Meanwhile they sent in no transport animals, although large sums had been handed over for their purchase. Our people were still immobile, and already, on the 18th, there had occurred a fall of snow several inches deep.

The Envoy was engaged in strange and dubious intrigues, and since the Afghans were not fulfilling their share of the treaty obligations, he appears to have regarded himself as no longer bound by its conditions, and free to try to obtain better terms from other sources, in pursuit of which purpose he was expending money in a variety of directions. The dark and unscrupulous Mohun Lal was his confidant and instrument. Akbar Khan and the chiefs of his party had become aware of Macnaghten's machinations, and they laid a snare for him into which he fell with open eyes. Emissaries were sent to him with the sinister proposals that the British should remain in Afghanistan until the spring, when they were to withdraw as of their own accord;

that the head of Ameenoolla Khan, one of the most powerful and obnoxious of the rebel leaders, should be presented
to the Envoy in return for a stipulated sum of money; and
that for all those services the British Government should
require Akbar Khan with a present of thirty lakhs of rupees,
and an annual pension of four lakhs. Macnaghten refused
peremptorily the proffer of Ameenoolla's head, but did not
reject co-operation in that chiefs capture by a dubious de-
vice in which British troops were to participate; he did not
hesitate to accept the general terms of the proposals; and he
consented to hold a conference with Akbar Khan on the
following day to carry into effect the projected measures.

On the morning of the 23d the deceived and doomed
man, accompanied by his staff-officers, Lawrence, Trevor
and Mackenzie, rode out from cantonments to keep the
fateful tryst on the bank of the Cabul river. His manner
was 'distracted and hurried.' When he told Lawrence of the
nature of the affair on which he was going, that shrewd
officer immediately warned him that it was a plot against
him. 'A plot!' he replied hastily, 'let me alone for that; trust
me for that!' and Lawrence desisted from useless expostula-
tion. Poor old Elphinstone had scented treachery; but the
Envoy had closed his mouth with the impatient words: 'I
understand these things better than you!' As he rode out, he
admitted the danger of the enterprise, but argued that if it
succeeded it was worth all risks. 'At all events,' he ended, 'let
the loss be what it may, I would rather die a hundred deaths
than live the last six weeks over again.' The escort halted,
and the four British gentlemen advanced to the place of
rendezvous, whither came presently Akbar Khan and his
party. Akbar began the conference by asking the Envoy if he
was ready to carry out the proposals presented to him over-
night. 'Why not?' was Sir William's short reply. A number
of Afghans, armed to the teeth, had gradually formed a cir-

cle around the informal durbar. Lawrence and Mackenzie pointed out this environment to some of the chiefs, who affected to drive off the intruders with their whips; but Akbar observed that it did not matter, as they 'were all in the secret.' 'Suddenly,' wrote Mackenzie, 'I heard Akbar call out, "Begeer! begeer!" ("Seize! seize!") and turning round I saw him grasp the Envoy's left hand with an expression on his face of the most diabolical ferocity. I think it was Sultan Jan who laid hold of the Envoy's right hand. They dragged him in a stooping posture down the hillock, the only words I heard poor Sir William utter being, "Az barae Khooda" ("For God's sake"). I saw his face, however, and it was full of horror and astonishment.' Neither Mackenzie nor Lawrence, the surviving companions of the Envoy, witnessed the actual end. 'Whether,' writes Kaye, 'he died on the spot, or whether he was slain by the infuriated ghazees, is not very clearly known; but the fanatics threw themselves on the prostrate body and hacked it with their knives.' There is no doubt that the head of the unfortunate Macnaghten was paraded in triumph through the streets of Cabul, and that the mangled trunk, after being dragged about the city, was hung up in the great bazaar. Of the three officers who accompanied the Envoy to the conference, Trevor was massacred, Lawrence and Mackenzie were saved with difficulty by friendly chiefs, and brought into the city, where they and Captain Skinner joined the hostages, Captains Connolly and Airey, under the safe roof of the venerable Mahomed Zemaun Khan.

That Akbar and the confederate chiefs spread a snare for the Envoy is plain, and that they regarded his acceptance of their deceitful proposals as a proof of his faithlessness to the treaty obligations to which he had bound himself. It was no element in their reasoning that since they had not regarded the treaty the British functionary might without breach of faith hold that it did not bind him. But it is improbable that the murder of Macnaghten was actually included in their scheme of action. Their intention seems to have been to seize him as a hostage, with intent thus to secure the evacuation of Afghanistan and the restoration of Dost Mahomed. The ill-fated Envoy's expressions on his way to the rendezvous indicate his unhinged state of mind. He went forth to sure treachery; Akbar's gust of sudden fury converted the planned abduction into savage murder, and his abrupt pistol bullet baulked the more wily and less ruthless project which had probably been devised in cold blood.

The escort brought back into cantonments tidings that the Envoy had been seized. The garrison got under arms, and remained passive throughout the day. The defences were manned at night, in the apprehension that the noise and disturbance in the city portended an assault; but that clamour was caused by the mustering of the Afghans in expectation that the British would attack the city, bent on vengeance on the murderers of the Envoy. Action of that nature was, however, wholly absent from the prostrate minds of the military chiefs. On the following afternoon Captain Lawrence transmitted certain overtures from the chiefs, as the result of a conference held by them, when, notwithstanding severe comments on the conduct of the Envoy, professions were made of sincere regret for his death. With certain alterations and additions, the treaty drawn up by Macnaghten was taken by the chiefs as the basis for the negotiations which they desired to renew. Major Pottinger, as now the senior 'political' with the force, was called on by General Elphinstone to undertake the task of conducting negotiations with the Afghan leaders. The high-souled Pottinger rose at the summons from the sickbed to which he had been confined ever since his wonderful escape from Charikar, and accepted the thankless and distasteful duty. It is not necessary to recount the details of negotiations, every article and every stage of which display the arrogance of the men who knew themselves masters of the situation, and reveal not less the degrading humiliation to which was submitting itself a strong brigade of British troops, whose arms were still in the soldiers' hands, and over whose ranks hung banners blazoned with victories that shall be memorable down the ages. On the sombre and cheerless Christmas Day Pottinger rose in the council of men who wore swords, and remonstrated with soldierly vigour and powerful argument against the degrading terms which the chiefs had contumeliously thrown to them. He produced letters from Jellalabad and Peshawur giving information of reinforcements on the way from India, and urging the maintenance of resistance. He argued that to conclude a treaty with the Afghans would be a fatal error, and suggested two alternative courses which offered a prospect of saving their honour and part of the army—the occupation of the Balla Hissar, which was the preferable measure, or the abandonment of camp, baggage, and encumbrances, and forcing a retreat down the passes. The council—Pottinger must have written sarcastically when he termed it a 'council of war'—unanimously decided that to remain in Cabul and to force a retreat were alike impracticable, and that nothing remained but the endeavour to release the army by agreeing to the conditions offered by the enemy. 'Under these circumstances,' in the words of Pottinger, 'as the Major-General coincided with the officers of the council, and refused to attempt occupying the Balla Hissar, and as his second in command declared that impracticable, I considered it my duty, notwithstanding my repugnance to and disapproval of the measure, to yield, and attempt to carry on a negotiation.'

This Pottinger accordingly did. The first demand with which he had to comply was to give bills for the great

sums promised by the Envoy to the chiefs for their services in furthering and supporting his treaty. This imposi-
tion had to be submitted to, since the Afghans stopped
the supplies until the extortion was complied with. The
next concession required was the surrender of the artillery of the force, with the exception of six field and three
mule guns; and the military chiefs endured this humiliation, against which even the demoralised soldiery chafed.
Then the demand for hostages had to be complied with,
and four officers were sent on to join the two hostages
already in Afghan hands. The chiefs had demanded four
married hostages, with their wives and children, and a
circular was sent round offering to volunteers the induce-
ment of a large stipend; but the sentiment of repulsion
was too strong to be overcome by the bribe. The sick and
wounded who could not bear the march were sent into
the city in accordance with an article of the treaty, two
surgeons accompanying their patients.

The treaty, ratified by the leading chiefs and sent into
cantonments on New Year's Day 1842, provided that the
British troops, within twenty-four hours after receiving
transport, and under the protection of certain chiefs and
an adequate escort, should begin their march of evacuation, the Jellalabad garrison moving down to Peshawur
in advance; that the six hostages left in Cabul should be
well treated, and liberated on the arrival at Peshawur of
Dost Mahomed; the sick and wounded left behind to be
at liberty to return to India on their recovery; all small
arms and ordnance stores in the cantonment magazine
to be made over to the Afghans 'as a token of friendship,'
on which account also, they were to have all the British
cannon except as above mentioned; the Afghans to escort
the Ghuznee garrison in safety to Peshawur; and a further
stipulation was that the British troops in Candahar and

Western Afghanistan were to resign the territories occupied by them and start quickly for India, provisioned and protected from molestation by the way.

Severe and humiliating as were those terms, they were not obtained without difficulty. The terms put forward in the earlier drafts of the treaty were yet more exacting, and the tone of the demands was abrupt, contemptuous, and insulting. Pottinger had to plead, to entreat, to be abject; to beg the masterful Afghans 'not to overpower the weak with sufferings'; 'to be good enough to excuse the women from the suffering' of remaining as hostages; and to entreat them 'not to forget kindness' shown by us in former days. One blushes not for but with the gallant Pottinger, loyally carrying out the miserable duty put upon him. The shame was not his; it lay on the council of superior officers, who overruled his remonstrances, and ground his face into the dust.

Our people were made to pass under the yoke every hour of their wretched lives during those last winter days in the Cabul cantonments. The fanatics and the common folk of the city and its environs swarmed around our petty ramparts, with their foul sneers and their blackguard taunts, hurled with impunity from where they stood at the muzzles of the loaded guns which the gunners were forbidden to fire. Officers and rank and file were in a condition of smouldering fury, but no act of reprisal or retribution was permitted. If the present was one continuous misery, the future lowered yet more gloomily. It was of common knowledge as well in the cantonments as in the city, that the engagements made by the chiefs were not worth the paper on which they had been written, and that treachery was being concerted against the force on its impending travail through the passes. It was told by a chief to one of the officers who was his friend, that Akbar Khan had sworn to have in his possession the British ladies as security for the safe restoration of his own family and relatives, and, strange forecast to be fulfilled almost to the very letter, had vowed to annihilate every soldier of the British army with the exception of one man, who should reach Jellalabad to tell the story of the massacre of all his comrades. Pottinger was well aware how desperate was the situation of the hapless people on whose behalf he had bent so low his proud soul. Mohun Lal warned him of the treachery the chiefs were plotting, and assured him that unless their sons should accompany the army as hostages, it would be attacked on the march. Day after day the departure was delayed, on the pretext that the chiefs had not completed their preparations for the safe conduct of the force and its encumbrances. Day after day the snow was falling with a quiet, ruthless persistency. The bitter night frosts were destroying the sepoys and the camp followers, their vitality weakened by semi-starvation and by the lack of firewood which had long distressed them. At length on January 5th, Sturt the engineer officer got his instructions to throw down into the ditch a section of the eastern rampart, and so furnish a freer exit than the gates could afford. The supply of transport was inadequate, provisions were scant, and the escort promised by the chiefs was not forthcoming. Pottinger advised waiting yet a little longer, until supplies and escort should arrive; but for once the military chiefs were set against the policy of delay, and firm orders were issued that the cantonments should be evacuated on the following day.

Shah Soojah remained in Cabul. The resolution became him better than anything else we know of the unfortunate man. It may be he reasoned that he had a chance for life by remaining in the Balla Hissar, and that from what he knew, there was no chance of life for anyone participating in the fateful march. He behaved fairly by the British authorities, sending more than one solemn warning pressing on them the occupation of the Balla Hissar. And there was some dignity in his appeal to Brigadier Anquetil, who commanded his own contingent, 'if it were well to forsake him in the hour of need, and to deprive him of the aid of that force which he had hitherto been taught to regard as his own?'

CHAPTER 7

The Catastrophe

The ill-omened evacuation by our doomed people of the cantonments wherein for two months they had undergone every extremity of humiliation and contumely, was begun on the dreary winter morning of January 6th, 1842. Snow lay deep on plain and hill-side; the cruel cold, penetrating through the warmest clothing, bit fiercely into the debilitated and thinly clad frames of the sepoys and the great horde of camp followers. The military force which marched out of cantonments consisted of about 4500 armed men, of whom about 690 were Europeans, 2840 native soldiers on foot, and 970 native cavalrymen. The gallant troop of Company's Horse-Artillery marched out with its full complement of six guns, to which, with three pieces of the mountain train, the artillery arm of the departing force was restricted by the degrading terms imposed by the Afghan chiefs. In good heart and resolutely commanded, a body of disciplined troops thus constituted, and of a fighting strength so respectable, might have been trusted not only to hold its own against Afghan onslaught, but if necessary to take the offensive with success. But alas, the heart of the hapless force had gone to water, its discipline was a wreck, its chiefs were feeble and apathetic; its steps were dogged by the incubus of some 12,000 camp followers, with a great company of women and children. The awful fate brooded over its forlorn banners of expiating by its utter annihilation, the wretched folly and sinister prosecution of the enterprise whose deserved failure was to be branded yet deeper on the gloomiest page of our national history, by the impending catastrophe of which the dark shadow already lay upon the blighted column.

The advance began to move out from cantonments at nine A.M. The march was delayed at the river by the noncompletion of the temporary bridge, and the whole of the advance was not across until after noon. The main body under Shelton, which was accompanied by the ladies, invalids, and sick, slowly followed. It as well as the advance was disorganised from the first by the throngs of camp followers with the baggage, who could not be prevented from mixing themselves up with the troops. The Afghans occupied the cantonments as portion after portion was evacuated by our people, rending the air with their exulting cries, and committing every kind of atrocity. It was late in the afternoon before the long train of camels following the main body had cleared the cantonments; and meanwhile the rear-guard was massed outside, in the space between the rampart and the canal, among the chaos of already abandoned baggage. It was exposed there to a vicious jezail fire poured into it by the Afghans, who abandoned the pleasures of plunder and arson for the yet greater joy of slaughtering the Feringhees. When the rear-guard moved away in the twilight, an officer and fifty men were left dead in the snow, the victims of the Afghan fire from the rampart of the cantonment; and owing to casualties in the gun teams it had been found necessary to spike and abandon two of the horse-artillery guns.

The rear-guard, cut into from behind by the pestilent ghazees, found its route encumbered with heaps of abandoned baggage around which swarmed Afghan plunder-

GHUZNEE

ers. Other Afghans, greedier for blood than for booty, were hacking and slaying among the numberless sepoys and camp followers who had dropped out of the column, and were lying or sitting on the wayside in apathetic despair, waiting for death and careless whether it came to them by knife or by cold. Babes lay on the snow abandoned by their mothers, themselves prostrate and dying a few hundred yards further on. It was not until two o'clock of the following morning that the rear-guard reached the straggling and chaotic bivouac in which its comrades lay in the snow at the end of the first short march of six miles. Its weary progress had been illuminated by the conflagration raging in the cantonments, which had been fired by the Afghan fanatics, rabid to erase every relic of the detested unbelievers.

It was a night of bitter cold. Out in the open among the snow, soldiers and camp followers, foodless, fireless, and shelterless, froze to death in numbers, and numbers more were frost-bitten. The cheery morning noise of ordinary camp life was unheard in the mournful bivouac. Captain Lawrence outlines a melancholy picture. 'The silence of the men betrayed their despair and torpor. In the morning I found lying close to me, stiff, cold, and quite dead, in full regimentals, with his sword drawn in his hand, an old grey-haired conductor named Macgregor, who, utterly exhausted, had lain down there silently to die.' Already defection had set in. One of the Shah's infantry regiments and his detachment of sappers and miners had deserted bodily, partly during the march of the previous day, partly in the course of the night.

No orders were given out, no bugle sounded the march, on the morning of the 7th. The column heaved itself forward sluggishly, a mere mob of soldiers, camp followers and cattle, destitute of any semblance of order or discipline. Quite half the sepoys were already unfit for duty; in hundreds they drifted in among the non-combatants and increased the confusion. The advance of the previous day was now the rear-guard. After plundering the abandoned baggage, the Afghans set to harassing the rear-guard, whose progress was delayed by the disorderly multitude blocking the road in front. The three mountain guns, temporarily separated from the infantry, were captured by a sudden Afghan rush. In vain Anquetil strove to rouse the 44th to make an effort for their recapture. Green was more successful with his handful of artillerymen, who followed him and the Brigadier and spiked the pieces, but being unsupported were compelled a second time to abandon them. On this march it became necessary also, from the exhaustion of their teams, to spike and abandon two more of the horse-artillery guns; so that there now remained with the force only a couple of six-pounders. While the rear-guard was in action, a body of Afghan horse charged on the flank, right into the heart of the baggage column, swept away much plunder, and spread confusion and dismay far and wide. The rear of the column would probably have been entirely cut off, but that reinforcements from the advance under Shelton pushed back the enemy, and by crowning the lateral heights kept open the thoroughfare. At Bootkhak was found Akbar Khan, who professed to have been commissioned to escort the force to Jellalabad, and who blamed our people for having marched out prematurely from the cantonments. He insisted on the halt of the column at Bootkhak until the following morning, when he would provide supplies, but he demanded an immediate subsidy of 15,000 rupees, and that Pottinger, Lawrence and Mackenzie should be given up to him as hostages that the force would not march beyond Tezeen until tidings should arrive that Sale had evacuated Jellalabad. Those officers by the General's instructions joined the Afghan chief on the following morning, and Akbar's financial requisition was obsequiously fulfilled. After two days' marching our people, who had brought out with them provisions for but five and a half days, expecting within that time to reach Jellalabad, were only ten miles forward on their march.

Another night passed, with its train of horrors—starvation, cold, exhaustion, death. Lady Sale relates that scarcely any of the baggage now remained; that there was no food for man or beast; that snow lay a foot deep on the ground; that even water from the adjacent stream was difficult to obtain, as the carriers were fired on in fetching it; and that she thought herself fortunate in being sheltered in a small tent in which 'we slept nine, all touching each other.' Daylight brought merely a more bitter realisation of utter misery. Eyre expresses his wonderment at the effect of two nights' exposure to the frost in disorganising the force. 'It had so nipped even the strongest men as to completely prostrate their powers and incapacitate them for service; even the cavalry, who suffered less than the rest, were obliged to be lifted on their horses.' In fact, only a few hundred serviceable men remained. At the sound of hostile fire the living struggled to their feet from their lairs in the snow, stiffened with cold, all but unable to move or hold a weapon, leaving many of their more fortunate comrades stark in death. A turmoil of confusion reigned. The Afghans were firing into the rear of the mass, and there was a wild rush of camp followers to the front, who stripped the baggage cattle of their loads and carried the animals off, leaving the ground strewn with ammunition, treasure, plate, and other property. The ladies were no longer carried in litters and palanquins, for their bearers were mostly dead; they sat in the bullet fire packed into panniers slung on camels, invalids as some of them were—one poor lady with her baby only five days old. Mess stores were being recklessly distributed, and Lady Sale honestly acknowledges that, as she sat on her horse in the cold, she felt very grateful for a tumbler of sherry, which at any other time would have made her 'very unladylike,' but which now merely warmed her. Cups full of sherry were drunk by young children without in the least affecting their heads, so strong on them was the hold of the cold.

It was not until noon that the living mass of men and animals was once more in motion. The troops were in utter disorganisation; the baggage was mixed up with the advance guard; the camp followers were pushing ahead in precipitate panic. The task before the wretched congeries of people was to thread the stupendous gorge of the Khoord Cabul pass—a defile about five miles long, hemmed in on either hand by steeply scarped hills. Down the bottom of the ravine dashed a mountain torrent, whose edges were lined with thick layers of ice, on which had formed glacier-like masses of snow. The 'Jaws of Death' were barely entered when the slaughter began. With the advance rode several Afghan chiefs, whose followers, by their command, shouted to the Ghilzais lining the heights to hold their fire, but the tribesmen gave no heed to the mandate. Lady Sale rode with the chiefs. The Ghilzai fire at fifty yards was close and deadly. The men of the advance fell fast. Lady Sale had a bullet in her arm, and three more through her dress. But the weight of the hostile fire fell on the main column, the baggage escort, and the rear-guard. Some of the ladies, who mostly were on camels which were led with the column, had strange adventures. On one camel was quite a group. In one of its panniers were Mrs Boyd and her little son, in the other Mrs Mainwaring, with her own infant and Mrs Anderson's eldest child. The camel fell, shot. A Hindustanee trooper took up Mrs Boyd *en croupe*, and carried her through in safety; another horseman behind whom her son rode, was killed, and the boy fell into Afghan hands. The Anderson girl shared the same fate. Mrs Mainwaring, with her baby in her arms, attempted to mount a baggage pony, but the load upset, and she pursued her way on foot. An Afghan horseman rode at her, threatened her with his sword, and tried to drag away the shawl in which she carried her child. She was rescued by a sepoy grenadier, who shot the Afghan dead, and then conducted the poor lady along the pass through the dead and dying, through, also, the close fire which struck down people near to her, almost to the exit of the pass, when a bullet killed the chivalrous sepoy, and Mrs Mainwaring had to continue her tramp to the bivouac alone.

A very fierce attack was made on the rear-guard, consisting of the 44th. In the narrow throat of the pass the regiment was compelled to halt by a block in front, and in this stationary position suffered severely. A flanking fire told heavily on the handful of European infantry. The belated stragglers masked their fire, and at length the soldiers fell back, firing volleys indiscriminately into the stragglers and the Afghans. Near the exit of the pass a commanding position was maintained by some detachments which still held together, strengthened by the only gun now remaining, the last but one having been abandoned in the gorge. Under cover of this stand the rear of the mass gradually drifted forward while the Afghan pursuit was checked, and at length all the surviving force reached the camping ground. There had been left dead in the pass about 500 soldiers and over 2500 camp followers.

Akbar and the chiefs, taking the hostages with them, rode forward on the track of the retreating force. Akbar professed that his object was to stop the firing, but Mackenzie writes that Pottinger said to him: 'Mackenzie, remember if I am killed that I heard Akbar Khan shout "Slay them!" in Pushtoo, although in Persian he called out to stop the firing.' The hostages had to be hidden away from the ferocious ghazees among rocks in the ravine until near evening, when in passing through the region of the heaviest slaughter they 'came upon one sight of horror after another. All the bodies were stripped. There were children cut in two. Hindustanee women as well as men—some frozen to death, some literally chopped to pieces, many with their throats cut from ear to ear.'

Snow fell all night on the unfortunates gathered tentless on the Khoord Cabul camping ground. On the morning of the 9th the confused and disorderly march was resumed, but after a mile had been traversed a halt for the day was ordered at the instance of Akbar Khan, who sent into camp by Captain Skinner a proposal that the ladies and children, with whose deplorable condition he professed with apparent sincerity to sympathise, should be made over to his protection, and that the married officers should accompany their wives; he pledging himself to preserve the party from further hardships and dangers, and afford its members safe escort through the passes in rear of the force. The General had little faith in the Sirdar, but he was fain to give his consent to an arrangement which promised alleviation to the wretchedness of the ladies, scarce any of whom had tasted a meal since leaving Cabul. Some, still weak from childbirth, were nursing infants only a few days old; other poor creatures were momentarily apprehending the pangs of motherhood. There were invalids whose only attire, as they rode in the camel panniers or shivered on the snow, was the nightdresses they wore when leaving the cantonments in their palanquins, and none possessed anything save the clothes on their backs. It is not surprising, then, that dark and doubtful as was the future to which they were consigning themselves, the ladies preferred its risks and chances to the awful certainties which lay before the doomed column. The Afghan chief had cunningly made it a condition of his proffer that the husbands should accompany their wives, and if there was a struggle in the breasts of the former between public and private duties, the General humanely decided the issue by ordering them to share the fortunes of their families.

Akbar Khan sent in no supplies, and the march was resumed on the morning of the both by a force attenuated by starvation, cold, and despair, diminished further by extensive desertion. After much exertion the advance, consisting of all that remained of the 44th, the solitary gun, and a detachment of cavalry, forced a passage to the front through the rabble of camp followers, and marched unmolested for about two miles until the Tunghee Tariki was reached, a deep gorge not more than ten feet wide. Men fell fast in the horrid defile, struck down by the Afghan fire from the heights; but the pass, if narrow, was short, and the advance having struggled through it moved on to the halting-place at Kubbar-i-Jubbar, and waited there for the arrival of the main body. But that body was never to emerge from out the shambles in the narrow throat of the Tunghee Tariki. The advance was to learn from the few stragglers who reached it the ghastly truth that it now was all that remained of the strong brigade which four days before had marched out from the Cabul cantonments. The slaughter from the Afghan fire had blocked the gorge with dead and dying. The Ghilzai tribesmen, at the turn into the pen at the other end of which was the blocked gorge, had closed up fiercely. Then the steep slopes suddenly swarmed with Afghans rushing sword in hand down to the work of butchery, and the massacre stinted not while living victims remained. The rear-guard regiment of sepoys was exterminated, save for two or three desperately wounded officers who contrived to reach the advance.

The remnant of the army consisted now of about seventy files of the 44th, about 100 troopers, and a detachment of horse-artillery with a single gun. The General sent to Akbar Khan to remonstrate with him on the attack he had allowed to be made after having guaranteed that the force should meet with no further molestation. Akbar protested his regret, and pleaded his inability to control the wild Ghilzai hillmen, over whom, in their lust for blood and plunder, their own chiefs had lost all control; but he was willing to guarantee the safe conduct to Jellalabad of the European officers and men if they would lay down their arms and commit themselves wholly into his hands. This sinister proposal the General refused, and the march was continued, led in disorder by the remnant of the camp followers. In the steep descent from the Huft Kotul into the Tezeen ravine, the soldiers following the rabble at some distance, came suddenly on a fresh butchery. The Afghans had suddenly fallen on the confused throng, and the descent was covered with dead and dying.

During the march from Kubbar-i-Jubbar to the Tezeen valley Shelton's dogged valour had mainly saved the force from destruction. With a few staunch soldiers of his own regiment, the one-armed veteran, restored now to his proper métier of stubborn fighting man, had covered the rear and repelled the Ghilzai assaults with persevering energy and dauntless fortitude. And he it was who now suggested, since Akbar Khan still held to his stipulation that the force should lay down its arms, that a resolute effort should be made to press on to Jugdulluk by a rapid night march of four-and-twenty miles, in the hope of clearing the passes in that vicinity before the enemy should have time to occupy them.

That the attempt would prove successful was doubtful, since the force was already exhausted; but it was the last

STORMING GHUZNEE

chance, and Shelton's suggestion was adopted. In the early moonlight the march silently began, an ill omen marking the start in the shape of the forced abandonment of the last gun. Fatal delay occurred between Seh Baba and Kutti Sung because of a panic among the camp followers, who, scared by a few shots, drifted backwards and forwards in a mass, retarding the progress of the column and for the time entirely arresting the advance of Shelton's and his rear-guard. The force could not close up until the morning, ten miles short of Jugdulluk, and already the Afghans were swarming on every adjacent height. All the way down the broken slope to Jugdulluk the little column trudged through the gauntlet of jezail fire which lined the road with dead and wounded. Shelton and his rear-guard handful performed wonders, again and again fending off with close fire and levelled bayonets the fierce rushes of Ghilzais charging sword in hand. The harassed advance reached Jugdulluk in the afternoon of the 11th, and took post behind some ruins on a height by the roadside, the surviving officers forming line in support of the gallant rear-guard struggling forward through its environment of assailants. As Shelton and his brave fellows burst through the cordon they were greeted by cheers from the knoll. But there was no rest for the exhausted people, for the Afghans promptly occupied commanding positions whence they maintained a fire from which the ruins afforded but scant protection. To men parched with thirst the stream at the foot of their knoll was but a tantalising aggravation, for to attempt to reach it was certain death. The snow they devoured only increased their sufferings, and but little stay was afforded by the raw flesh of a few gun bullocks. Throughout the day volley after volley was poured down upon the weary band by the inexorable enemy. Frequent sallies were made, and the heights were cleared, but the positions were soon reoccupied and the ruthless fire was renewed.

Captain Skinner, summoned by Akbar, brought back a message that General Elphinstone should visit him to take part in a conference, and that Brigadier Shelton and Captain Johnson should be given over as hostages for the evacuation of Jellalabad. Compliance was held to be imperative, and the temporary command was entrusted to Brigadier Anquetil. Akbar was extremely hospitable to his compulsory guests; but he insisted on including the General among his hostages, and was not moved by Elphinstone's representations that he would prefer death to the disgrace of being separated from his command in its time of peril. The Ghilzai chiefs came into conference burning with hatred against the British, and revelling in the anticipated delights of slaughtering them. Akbar seemed sincere in his effort to conciliate them, but was long unsuccessful. Their hatred seemed indeed stronger than their greed; but at length toward nightfall Akbar announced that pacific arrangements had been accepted by the tribes, and that what remained of the force should be allowed to march unmolested to Jellalabad.

How futile was the compact, if indeed there was any compact, was soon revealed. The day among the ruins on the knoll had passed in dark and cruel suspense—in hunger, thirst, and exhaustion, in the presence of frequent death; and as the evening fell, in anguish and all but utter despair. As darkness set in the conviction enforced itself that to remain longer in the accursed place was madness; and the little band, leaving behind perforce the sick and wounded, marched out, resolute to push through or die fighting. In the valley the only molestation at first was a desultory fire from the camping Ghilzais, who were rather taken by surprise, but soon became wide awake to their opportunities. Some hurried forward to occupy the pass rising from the valley to the Jugdulluk crest; others, hanging on the rear

and flanks of the column encumbered with its fatal incubus of camp followers, mixed among the unarmed throng
with their deadly knives, and killed and plundered with the
dexterity of long practice. Throughout the tedious march
up the steeply rising defile a spattering fire came from the
rocks and ridges flanking the track, all but blocked by the
surging concourse of miserable followers. The advance had
to employ cruel measures to force its way through the chaos toward the crest. As it is approached from the Jugdulluk direction the flanking elevations recede and merge in
the transverse ridge, which is crowned by a low-cut abrupt
rocky upheaval, worn down somewhat where the road
passes over the crest by the friction of traffic. Just here the
tribesmen had constructed a formidable abattis of prickly
brushwood, which stretched athwart the road, and dammed
back the fugitives in the shallow oval basin between the
termination of the ravine and the summit of the ridge. In
this trap were caught our hapless people and the swarm of
their native followers, and now the end was very near. From
behind the barrier, and around the lip of the great trap, the
hillmen fired their hardest into the seething mass of soldiers
and followers writhing in the awful Gehenna on which the
calm moon shone down. On the edges of this whirlpool
of death the fell Ghilzais were stabbing and hacking with
the ferocious industry inspired by thirst for blood and lust
for plunder. It is among the characteristics of our diverse-
natured race to die game, and even to thrill with a strange
fierce joy when hope of escape from death has all but passed
away and there remains only to sell life at the highest possible premium of exchange. Among our people, face to face
with death on the rocky Jugdulluk, officers and soldiers
alike fought with cool deadly rancour. The brigadier and
the private engaged in the same fierce mêlée , fought side
by side, and fell side by side. Stalwart Captain Dodgin of

the 44th slew five Afghans before he fell. Captain Nicholl of the horse-artillery, gunless now, rallied to him the few staunch gunners who were all that remained to him of his noble and historic troop, and led them on to share with him a heroic death.

All did not perish on the rugged summit of the Jugdulluk. The barrier was finally broken through, and a scant remnant of the force wrought out its escape from the slaughter-pit. Small detachments, harassed by sudden onslaughts, and delayed by reluctance to desert wounded comrades, were trudging in the darkness down the long slope to the Soorkhab. The morning of the 13th dawned near Gundamuk on the straggling group of some twenty officers and forty-five European soldiers. Its march arrested by sharp attacks, the little band moved aside to occupy a defensive position on an adjacent hillock. A local sirdar invited the senior officer to consult with him as to a pacific arrangement, and while Major Griffiths was absent on this errand there was a temporary suspension of hostilities. The Afghans meanwhile swarmed around the detachment with a pretence of friendship, but presently attempts were made to snatch from the soldiers their arms. This conduct was sternly resented, and the Afghans were forced back. They ascended an adjacent elevation and set themselves to the work of deliberately picking off officer after officer, man after man. The few rounds remaining in the pouches of the soldiers were soon exhausted, but the detachment stood fast, and calmly awaited the inevitable end. Rush after rush was driven back from its steadfast front, but at last, nearly all being killed or wounded, a final onset of the enemy, sword in hand, terminated the struggle, and completed the dismal tragedy. Captain Souter of the 44th, with three or four privates all of whom as well as himself were wounded, was spared and carried into captivity; he saved the colours of his regiment, which he had tied round his waist before leaving Jugdulluk. A group of mounted officers had pushed forward as soon as they had cleared the barrier on the crest. Six only reached Futtehabad in safety. There they were treacherously offered food, and while they halted a few moments to eat two were cut down. Of the four who rode away three were overtaken and killed within four miles of Jellalabad; one officer alone survived to reach that haven of refuge.

The ladies, the married officers, and the original hostages, followed Akbar Khan down the passes toward Jugdulluk, pursuing the line of retreat strewn with its ghastly tokens of slaughter, and recognising almost at every step the bodies of friends and comrades. At Jugdulluk they found General Elphinstone, Brigadier Shelton, and Captain Johnson, and learned the fate which had overtaken the marching force. On the following day Akbar quitted Jugdulluk with his hostages and the ladies, all of whom were virtually prisoners, and rode away through the mountains in a northerly direction. On the fourth day the fort of Budiabad in the Lughman valley was reached, where Akbar left the prisoners while he went to attempt the reduction of Jellalabad.

CHAPTER 8

The Siege and Defence of Jellalabad

Sale's brigade, retreating from Gundamuk, reached Jellalabad on the 12th November 1841. An investigation into the state of the fortifications of that place showed them, in their existing condition, to be incapable of resisting a vigorous assault. But it was resolved to occupy the place, and to Captain George Broadfoot, as garrison engineer, was committed the duty of making it defensible. This assuredly was no light task. The enciente was far too extensive for the slender garrison, and its tracing was radically bad. The ramparts were so dilapidated that in places they were scarcely discernible, and the ruins strewn over what should have been the glacis afforded near cover to assailants, whose attitude was already so threatening as to hinder the beginning of repairing operations. Their fire swept the defences, and their braves capered derisively to the strains of a bagpipe on the adjacent rocky elevation, which thenceforth went by the name of 'Piper's Hill.' A sortie on the 15th cleared the environs of the troublesome Afghans, supplies began to come in, and Broad-foot was free to set his sappers to the task of repairing the fortifications, in which work the entrenching tools he had wrenched from the Cabul stores proved invaluable. How greatly Sale had erred in shutting up his force in Jellalabad was promptly demonstrated. The connecting posts of Gundamuk and Peshbolak had to be evacuated; and thus, from Jumrood at the foot of the Khyber up to Cabul, there remained no intermediate post in British possession with the solitary exception of Jellalabad, and communications were entirely interrupted except through the medium of furtive messengers.

The Jellalabad garrison was left unmolested for nearly a fortnight, and the repairs were well advanced when on the 29th the Afghans came down, invested the place, and pushed their skirmishers close up to the walls. On December 1st Colonel Dennie headed a sortie, which worsted the besiegers with considerable slaughter and drove them from the vicinity. Bad news came at intervals from Cabul, and at the new year arrived a melancholy letter from Pottinger, confirming the rumours already rife of the murder of the Envoy, and of the virtual capitulation to which the Cabul force had submitted. A week later an official communication was received from Cabul, signed by General Elphinstone and Major Pottinger, formally announcing the convention which the Cabul force had entered into with the chiefs, and ordering the garrison of Jellalabad forthwith to evacuate that post and retire to Peshawur, leaving behind with 'the new Governor,' an Afghan chief who was the bearer of the humiliating missive, the fortress guns and such stores and baggage as there lacked transport to remove. The council of war summoned by Sale was unanimous in favour of non-compliance with this mandate. Broadfoot urged with vigour that an order by a superior who was no longer a free agent and who issued it under duress, could impose no obligation of obedience. Sale pronounced himself untrammelled by a convention forced from people 'with knives at their throats,' and was resolute in the expression of his determination to hold Jellalabad unless ordered by the Government to withdraw.

More and more ominous tidings poured in from Cabul.

A letter received on January both reported the Cabul force to be still in the cantonments, living utterly at the mercy of the Afghans; another arriving on the 12th told of the abandonment of the cantonments and the beginning of the march, but that the forlorn wayfarers were lingering in detention at Bootkhak, halted in their misery by the orders of Akbar Khan. Those communications in a measure prepared the people in Jellalabad for disaster, but not for the awful catastrophe of which Dr Brydon had to tell, when in the afternoon of the 13th the lone man, whose approach to the fortress Lady Butler's painting so pathetically depicts, rode through the Cabul gate of Jellalabad. Dr Brydon was covered with cuts and contusions, and was utterly exhausted. His first few hasty sentences extinguished all hope in the hearts of the listeners regarding their Cabul comrades and friends.

There was naturally great excitement in Jellalabad, but no panic. The working parties were called in, the assembly was sounded, the gates were closed, the walls were lined, and the batteries were manned; for it was believed for the moment that the enemy were in full pursuit of fugitives following in Brydon's track. The situation impressed Broadfoot with the conviction that a crisis had come in the fortunes of the Jellalabad garrison. He thought it his duty to lay before the General the conditions of the critical moment which he believed to have arrived, pointing out to him that the imperative alternatives were that he should either firmly resolve on the defence of Jellalabad to the last extremity, or that he should make up his mind to a retreat that very night, while as yet retreat was practicable. Sale decided on holding on to the place, and immediately announced to the Commander-in-Chief his resolve to persevere in a determined defence, relying on the promise of the earliest possible relief.

Dr. Brydon

Because of the defection of his Sikh auxiliaries and the faint-heartedness of his sepoys, Wild's efforts to cross the threshold of the Khyber had failed, and with the tidings of his failure there came to Sale the information that the effort for his relief must be indefinitely postponed. It may be assumed that this intimation weakened in some degree the General's expressed resolution to hold Jellalabad with determination, and it is not to be denied that this resolution was in a measure conditional on the not unwarranted expectation of early relief. Neither he nor his adviser Macgregor appears to have realised how incumbent on the garrison of Jellalabad it was to hold out to the last extremity, irrespective of consequences to itself, unless it should receive a peremptory recall from higher authority; or to have recognised the glorious opportunity presented of inspiriting by its staunch constancy and high-souled self-abnegation a weak government staggering under a burden of calamity. Than Sale no braver soldier ever wore sword, but a man may delight to head a forlorn hope and yet lack nerve to carry with high heart a load of responsibility; nor was Macgregor so constituted as to animate his chief to noble emprise. Fast on the heels of the gloomy tidings from the Khyber mouth there came to them from Shah Soojah, who was still the nominal sovereign at Cabul, a curt peremptory letter obviously written under compulsion, of which the following were the terms: 'Your people have concluded a treaty with us; you are still in Jellalabad; what are your intentions? Tell us quickly.'

Sale summoned a council of war, which assembled at his quarters on January 27th. Its proceedings were recorded, and the documents laid before it were preserved by Captain Henry Havelock in his capacity as Sale's staff-officer. Record and papers were reclaimed from Havelock's custody by General Sale before the evacuation of Afghanistan, and had been long lost to sight. They have recently been deposited among the records of the India Office, but not before their latest non-official possessor had published some extracts from them. It is to be hoped that the more important documents may be given to the public in full, since passages from documents, whether intentionally or not, may be so extracted as to be misleading. Broadfoot, who had been a member of the council of war, and who was apparently aware of the suppression of the official records, wrote in 1843 a detailed narrative of its proceedings while his recollection of them was still fresh, and this narrative he sent to Havelock, desiring him to note 'any points erroneously stated, distinguishing between what you may merely not remember and what you know I am mistaken in.' Havelock, who was a loyal and ardent admirer of General Sale, having sparsely annotated Broadfoot's narrative, returned it with the statement that he had compared it with memoranda still in his possession, and that he considered that it 'contributes a fair and correct statement of that which occurred.' The officers comprising the council to whom Sale and Macgregor addressed themselves were Colonel Dennie of the 13th, Colonel Monteath of the 35th N.I., Captains Backhouse and Abbott of the artillery, Captain Oldfield commanding the cavalry, and Captain Broadfoot the garrison engineer. The following is a summary of the proceedings, as recorded by Broadfoot and authenticated by Havelock.

After a few formal words from General Sale, he called on Macgregor to submit a matter on which that political officer and himself were agreed. Macgregor then described the situation from the point of view of Sale and himself, and expressed their united conviction that nothing was to be hoped for from the Government. Reserving his own liberty of action, he sought the opinion of the officers on offers received from Akbar Khan to treat for the evacuation of Afghanistan, and he laid before them a draft answer to Shah Soojah's curt letter, professing the readiness of the garrison to evacuate Jellalabad on his requisition, since it was held only for him, but naming certain conditions: the exchange of hostages, the restoration of British prisoners and hostages in exchange for the Afghan hostages on arrival of the force at Peshawur, escort thither 'in safety and honour,' with arms, colours, and guns, and adequate assistance of supplies and transport. Both Sale and Macgregor frankly owned that they were resolved to yield, and negotiate for safe retreat.

Great excitement from the first had pervaded the assemblage, and when Macgregor had finished his statement Broadfoot arose in his wrath. He declined to believe that the Government had abandoned the Jellalabad garrison to its fate, and there was a general outburst of indignation when Sale produced a letter carrying that significance. Broadfoot waxed so warm in his remonstrances against the proposed action that an adjournment was agreed to. Next day Sale and Macgregor urged that it was impossible to hold out much longer, that later retreat would be impracticable, and that the scheme they proposed was safe and honourable. Broadfoot denounced it as disgraceful, contended that they could hold Jellalabad indefinitely—'could colonise if they liked'—and retreat at discretion. He denied that the place was held for Shah Soojah, and challenged their right to surrender the post unless by Government order. Hostages he proclaimed worthless while the Afghans held heavier pledges of ours in the shape of prisoners and hostages. He denounced as disgraceful the giving of hostages on our part. Monteath's remark that nobody would go as a hostage roused Oldfield to express himself tersely but pointedly on the subject. 'I for one,' he exclaimed in great agitation, 'will fight here to the last drop of my blood, but I plainly declare that I will never be a hostage, and I am surprised that anyone should propose such a thing, or regard an Afghan's word as worth anything.' The resolution to treat for the abandonment of Jellalabad was carried, Oldfield only voting with Broadfoot against it, but the stipulations: regarding hostages were omitted. Broadfoot continued to press modifications of the conditions set out in the proposed reply, pleading, but in vain, that the restoration of the prisoners in Afghan hands before departure of the garrison should be insisted on; and that since evacuation was resolved on, it should at least be conducted as a military operation, and not degradingly under escort. Then, and little wonder, he objected to expressions in the draft letter as too abject, and he was successful in procuring the alteration of them. The letter was written out, signed by Macgregor, and despatched to Cabul. It was agreed that those members of the council who chose to do should record in writing the reasons for their votes, and this was done by Dennie, Monteath, Abbott, and Broadfoot.

Broadfoot, pending an answer from Cabul, set the garrison to work in digging a ditch round the fortifications. The reply from the Shah, to the effect 'If you are sincere in offers, let all the chief gentlemen affix their seals,' was laid before the reassembled council on February 12th. The implied imputation on the good faith of British officers might well have stung to indignation the meekest; but the council's opinion was taken as to the expediency of complying with the derogatory request made by the Shah, as well as of a stipulation—a modification of what Broadfoot had originally urged in vain—for the surrender of all prisoners, hostages, sick, and wounded under detention in Afghanistan, on the arrival at Peshawur of the Jellalabad brigade. The members of council, who in the long interval since the previous meeting had been gradually regaining their self-respect and mental equipoise, unanimously declined to accept the proposals tendered them by their commanding officer and his political ally; and a letter written by Monteath was accepted, which 'was not a continuation of the negotiation.'

Thus ended the deliberations of the memorable council of war, whose eleventh hour resolve to 'hold the fort' mainly averted the ruin of British prestige in India and throughout the regions bordering on our Eastern Empire; and the credit of its final decision to repudiate the humiliating proposals of Sale and Macgregor belongs to George Broadfoot, who was firmly though silently backed by Havelock. The day after that decision was formulated a letter came from Peshawur informing the garrison that every effort would be made for its relief; and thenceforth there was no more talk of surrender, nor was the courage of the little brigade impaired even when the earthquake of February 19th shook the newly repaired fortifications into wreck. Broadfoot's vehement energy infected the troops, and by the end of the month the parapets were entirely restored, the bastions repaired, and every battery re-established.

After the council of war had rejected the proposals laid before it, a decision which in effect involved the maintenance of the defence to the last extremity, nearly two months passed without the occurrence of any important event, except the speedily retrieved misfortune of the earthquake of February 19th. The close investment of the place by Akbar Khan thwarted the efforts of the foraging parties to obtain much needed supplies. Those efforts were not vigorous, for Sale, aware of his garrison's poverty of ammunition, was bent on a passive defence, and steadily refused his consent to vigorous sorties. The policy may have had its abstract merits, but it was certainly unsatisfactory in this respect, that perseverance in it involved the unpleasantness of apparently inevitable starvation. General Pollock had arrived in Peshawur, and was making energetic efforts to get his force in order for the accomplishment of the relief of Jellalabad. But he foresaw serious delays, and so late as the middle of March was still unable to specify with any definiteness the probable date of his arrival at that place. The European troops in Jellalabad would be out of meat rations early in April, and Havelock's calculation was that the grain, on which mainly subsisted the native soldiers, who had been on half rations since the new year, would be exhausted before the middle of that month. Sale modified his policy of inactivity when he learned that the blockading Afghans were attempting to drive a mine under a salient of the defences, and Dennie on March 11th led out a sally, destroyed the works, and thrust back Akbar's encroachments. The general lack of vigour, however, on the garrison's part emboldened the Afghans so much that they actually grazed their flocks of sheep within 600 yards of the walls. This was too impudent, and the General consented to a raid, which resulted in the acquisition of some 500 sheep, an invaluable addition to the commissariat resources. It is worth recording that the native regiment gave up its share of the sheep to the soldiers of the 13th, on the ground that Europeans needed animal food more than did natives of India.

On April 6th the Afghan leader fired a salute in triumph for a supposititious repulse of Pollock in the Khyber. In regard to what then happened there is a strange conflict of testimony. General Sale, in a private letter written six weeks later, states: 'I made my arrangements with Macgregor to sally the next day, provided we did not hear that Pollock had forced the pass.' Akbar's salutes, and the information of spies that Pollock had fallen back, 'made us look very grave—our case desperate, our provisions nearly out, and no relief at hand. I therefore decided to play a bold stroke to relieve ourselves, and give courage to Pollock's force in case of success. If we failed in thrashing Akbar, we would have left our bones on the field.' Abbott's diary of April 5th and 6th records that spies reported that Pollock had been repulsed at Ali Musjid, and that the heads of three of his officers had been sent in to Akbar, whereupon 'all the commanding officers waited on the General, beseeching him to attack Akbar instantly. The 13th and the battery got all ready for work, but the old General was obstinate, and refused to act.' Backhouse's diary (April 6th) mentions that Pollock having been reported repulsed, and Akbar having fired a salute, the officers commanding corps and detachments went in a body and proposed to the General to attack Akbar instantly, but without success. 'Immediately the matter was broached, the General set his face against anything of the kind, and disagreed about every point—insisted that the enemy had 5000 or 6000 men in camp, and were too strong for us; and then, the next minute, that it was no use going out as we couldn't punish them, as they wouldn't stand ; and concluding with usual excuse for inactivity, "It isn't our game." Words ran precious high....'

Whether spontaneously or under pressure, General Sale must have ordered a sortie in force; for at dawn of the 7th three infantry columns marched out by the Cabul gate, the right commanded by Havelock, the centre by Dennie, the left by Monteath, General Sale being in command of the whole force. Akbar, reputed about 5000 strong, was in formation in front of his camp about three miles west of Jellalabad, his left flank resting on the river, with an advanced post of 300 men in the 'patched up' fort about midway between his camp and Jellalabad. The prescribed tactics were to march straight on the enemy, with which Monteath and Havelock complied; but Dennie, whether with or without orders is a matter in dispute, diverged to assail the 'patched up' fort. The outer defences were carried, gallant old Dennie riding at the head of his men to receive his death wound. In vain did the guns for which Sale had sent batter at the inner keep, and the General abandoning the attempt to reduce it, led on in person the centre column. Meanwhile Havelock and Monteath had been moving steadily forward, until halted by orders when considerably advanced. Havelock had to form square once and again against the Afghan horsemen, who, however, did not dare to charge home. The artillery came to the front at the gallop, and poured shot and shell into Akbar's mass. The three columns, now abreast of each other, deployed into line, and moving forward at the double in the teeth of the Afghan musketry fire, swept the enemy clean out of his position, capturing his artillery, firing his camp, and putting him to utter rout. Akbar, by seven o'clock in the April morning, had been signally beaten in the open field by the troops he had boasted of blockading in the fortress.

The garrison of Jellalabad had thus wrought out its own relief. Thenceforth it experienced neither annoyance nor scarcity. Pollock arrived a fortnight after the dashing sally which had given the garrison deliverance, and the head of his column was played into its camp on the Jellalabad plain by the band of the 13th, to the significant tune 'Oh, but ye've been lang o'coming.' The magniloquent Ellenborough dubbed Sale's brigade 'the Illustrious Garrison,' and if the expression is overstrained, its conduct was without question eminently creditable.

CHAPTER 9
Retribution & Rescue

It was little wonder that the unexpected tidings of the Cabul outbreak, and the later shock of the catastrophe in the passes, should have temporarily unnerved the Governor-General. But Lord Auckland rallied his energies with creditable promptitude. His successor was on the voyage out, and in the remnant of his term that remained he could not do more than make dispositions which his successor might find of service. Every soldier of the 'Army of Retribution' was despatched to the frontier during Lord Auckland's rule. Lord Auckland appointed to the command of the troops which he was sending forward a quiet, steadfast, experienced officer of the artillery arm, who had fought under Lake at Deig and Bhurtpore, and during his forty years of honest service had soldiered steadily from the precipices of Nepaul to the rice-swamps of the Irrawaddy. Pollock was essentially the fitting man for the service that lay before him, characterised as he was by strong sense, shrewd sagacity, calm firmness, and self-command. When his superior devolved on him an undue onus of responsibility he was to prove himself thoroughly equal to the occasion, and the sedate, balanced man murmured not, but probably was rather amused when he saw a maker of phrases essaying to deck himself in his laurels. There were many things in Lord Auckland's Indian career of which it behoved him to repent, but it must go to his credit that he gave Pollock high command, and that he could honestly proclaim, as he made his preparations to quit the great possession whose future his policy had endangered, that he had contributed toward the retrieval of the crisis by promptly furthering 'such operations as might be required for the maintenance of the honour and interests of the British Government.'

Brigadier Wild reached Peshawur with a brigade of four sepoy regiments just before the new year. He was destitute of artillery, his sepoys were in poor heart, and the Sikh contingent was utterly untrustworthy. To force the Khyber seemed hopeless. Wild, however, made the attempt energetically enough. But the Sikhs mutinied, expelled their officers, and marched back to Peshawur; Wild's sepoys, behaving badly, were driven back with loss from the mouth of the pass, and Wild himself was wounded. When Pollock reached Peshawur on February 6th, 1842, he found half of Wild's brigade sick in hospital, and the whole of it in a state of utter demoralisation. A second brigade commanded by Brigadier-General McCaskill, had accompanied Pollock, the sepoys of which promptly fell under the evil influence of Wild's dispirited and disaffected regiments. Pollock had to resist the pressing appeals for speedy relief made to him from Jellalabad, and patiently to devote weeks and months to the restoration of the morale and discipline of the disheartened sepoys of his command, and to the reinvigoration of their physique. By kindness combined with firmness he was able gradually to inspire them with perfect trust and faith in him, and when in the end of March there reached him a third brigade, comprising British cavalry and horse-artillery, ordered forward by Lord Auckland on receipt of tidings of the destruction of the Cabul force, he felt himself at length justified in advancing with confidence.

Before daylight on the morning of April 5th Pollock's army about 8000 strong, consisting of eight infantry regiments, three cavalry corps, a troop and two batteries of artillery, and a mountain train, marched from the Jumrood camping ground into the portals of the Khyber. Pollock's scheme of operations was perfect in conception and complete in detail. His main column, with strong advance and rear-guards, was to pursue the usual road through the pass. It was flanked on each side by a chain of infantry detachments, whose assigned duty was to crown the heights and sweep them clear of assailants in advance of the head of the central column. The Afreedi hill men had blocked the throat of the pass by a formidable barrier, behind which they were gathered in force, waiting for the opportunity which was never to come to them. For the main body of Pollock's force serenely halted, while the flanking columns, breaking into skirmishing order, hurried in the grey dawn along the slopes and heights, dislodging the Afreedi pickets as they advanced, driving them before them with resolute impetuosity, and pushing forward so far as to take in reverse with their concentrated fire the great barrier and its defenders. The clansmen, recognising the frustration of their devices, deserted the position in its rear, and rushed tumultuously away to crags and sungahs where knife and jezail might still be plied. The centre column then advanced unmolested to the deserted barricade, through which the sappers soon cleared a thoroughfare. The guns swept with shrapnel the hill-sides in front, the flanking detachments pushed steadily further and yet further forward, chasing and slaying the fugitive hillmen; and the Duke of Wellington's observation was that morning fully made good, that he had never heard that our troops were not equal, as well in their personal activity as in their arms, to contend with and overcome any natives of hills whatever.' The whole British force, in its order of three columns, the centre in the bed of the hollow, the wings on the flanking ridges, steadily if slowly moved on in the assured consciousness of victory. It was sunset before the rear-guard was in camp under the reoccupied Ali Musjid. The Sikh troops who were to keep open Pollock's communications with Peshawur moved simultaneously on Ali Musjid by a more circuitous route.

While Pollock was halted opposite the throat of the Khyber waiting for the demolition of the Afreedi barricade, the ill-starred Shah Soojah was being murdered, on his way from the Balla Hissar of Cabul to review on the Siah Sung slopes the reinforcements which Akbar Khan was clamouring that he should lead down to aid that Sirdar in reducing Jellalabad before relief should arrive. Ever since the outbreak of November Shah Soojah had led a dog's life. He had reigned in Cabul, but he had not ruled. The Sirdars dunned him for money, and jeered at his protestations of poverty. It is not so much a matter of surprise that he should have been murdered as that, feeble, rich, and loathed, he should have been let live so long. It does not seem worth while to discuss the vexed question whether or not he was faithful to his British allies. He was certainly entitled to argue that he owed us nothing, since what we did in regard to him was nakedly for our own purposes. Shah Soojah's second son Futteh Jung had himself proclaimed his father's successor. The vicissitudes of his short reign need not be narrated. While Pollock was gathering his brigades at Gundamuk in the beginning of the following September, a forlorn Afghan, in dirty and tattered rags, rode into his camp. This scarecrow was Futteh Jung, who, unable to endure longer his sham kingship and the ominous tyranny of Akbar Khan, had fled from Cabul in disguise to beg a refuge in the British camp.

Pollock's march from Ali Musjid to Jellalabad was slow, but almost unmolested. He found, in his own words, 'the fortress strong, the garrison healthy; and except for wine and beer, better off than we are.' One principal object of his commission had been accomplished; he had relieved the garrison of Jellalabad, and was in a position to ensure its safe withdrawal. But his commission gave him a considerable discretion, and a great company of his countrymen and countrywomen were still in Afghan durance. The calm pulsed, resolute commander had views of his own as to his duty, and he determined in his patient, steadfast way to tarry a while on the Jellalabad plain, in the hope that the course of events might play into his hands.

Maclaren's brigade, which in the beginning of November 1841 General Elphinstone had instructed General Nott to despatch with all speed to Cabul, returned to Candahar early in December. Nott in despatching it had deferred reluctantly to superior authority, and probably Maclaren not sorry to have in the snowfall a pretext for retracing his steps. Atta Mahomed Khan, sent from Cabul to foment mischief in the Candahar regions, had gathered to his banner a considerable force. General Nott quietly waited until the Sirdar, at the head of some 10,000 men, came within five miles of Candahar, and then he crushed him after twenty minutes' fighting. The fugitives found refuge in the camp of the disaffected Dooranee chiefs, whose leader Meerza Ahmed was sedulously trying to tamper with Nott's native troops, severe weather hindering the General from attacking him. Near the end of February there reached Nott a letter two months old from Elphinstone and Pottinger, ordering him to evacuate Candahar and retire to India, in pursuance of the convention into which they had entered. The Dooranee chiefs astutely urged that Shah Soojah, no longer supported by British bayonets, was now ruling in Cabul, as an argument in favour of Nott's withdrawal. Nott's answer was brief: 'I will not treat with any person whatever for the retirement of the British troops from Afghanistan, until I have received instructions from the Supreme Government'—a blunt sentence in curious contrast to the missive which Sale and Macgregor laid before the Jellalabad council of war. When presently there came a communication from Government intimating that the continued occupation of Candahar was regarded as conducive to the interest of the state, Nott and Rawlinson were in a position to congratulate themselves on having anticipated the wishes of their superiors. The situation, however, became so menacing that early in March its Afghan inhabitants were expelled from the city of Candahar to the last soul; and then Nott, leaving a garrison in the place, took the field in force. The old soldier, wary as he was, became the victim of Meerza's wily strategy. As he advanced, the Afghans retired, skirmishing assiduously. Leaving Nott in the Turnuk valley, they doubled back on Candahar, and in the early darkness of the night of the 10th March they furiously assailed the city gates. They fired one of the gates, and the swarming ghazees tore down with fury its blazing planks and the red-hot ironwork. The garrison behaved valiantly. Inside the burning gate they piled up a rampart of grain bags, on which they trained a couple of guns loaded with case. For three hours after the gate fell did the fanatics hurl assault after assault on the interior barricade. They were terribly critical hours, but the garrison prevailed, and at midnight, with a loss of many hundreds, the obstinate assailants sullenly drew off. Nott, although urgently summoned, was unable to reach Candahar until the 12th.

Candahar was fortunately preserved, but at the end of March the unpleasant tidings came that Ghuznee, which British valour had carried by storm three years before, had

The Last Stand

now reverted into Afghan possession. The siege had lasted for nearly three and a half months. In mid-December the besiegers occupied the city in force, introduced by the citizens through a subterranean way; and the garrison, consisting chiefly of a regiment of sepoys, withdrew into the citadel. The bitter winter and the scant rations took the heart out of the natives of the warm and fertile Indian plains; but nevertheless it was not until March 6th that the garrison, under pledge of being escorted to Peshawur with colours, arms, and baggage, marched out. The unfortunates would have done better to have died a soldierly death, with arms in their hands and the glow of fighting in their hearts. As the event was, faith with them was broken, and save for a few officers who were made prisoners, most were slaughtered, or perished in a vain attempt to escape.

During his long isolation Nott's resources had been seriously depleted, and he had ordered up from Scinde a brigade, escorting much needed treasure, ammunition, and medicines. Brigadier England was entrusted with the command of this force, whose assemblage at Quetta was expected about the end of March. Pending its gathering England had moved out toward the entrance of the Kojuk Pass, where he met with a sharp and far from creditable repulse, and fell back on Quetta miserably disheartened, suggesting in his abjectness that Nott should abandon Candahar and retire on him. The stout old soldier at Candahar waxed wroth at the limpness of his subordinate, and addressed to England a biting letter, ordering peremptorily the latter's prompt advance to Candahar, engaging to dry-nurse him through the Kojuk by a brigade sent down from Candahar for the purpose, and remarking sarcastically, 'I am well aware that war cannot be made without loss; but yet perhaps British troops can oppose Asiatic armies without defeat.' Thus exhorted England moved, to find his march through the

Kojuk protected by Wymer's sepoys from Candahar, who had crowned the lateral heights before he ventured into the pass; and he reached Candahar without maltreatment on the 10th May, bringing to Nott the much needed supplies which rendered that resolute man equal to any enterprise.

It remained, however, to be seen whether any enterprise was to be permitted to him and to his brother commander lying in camp on the Jellalabad plain. Lord Ellenborough, the successor of Lord Auckland, had struck a firm if somewhat inexplicit note in his earliest manifesto, dated March 13th. A single sentence will indicate its tenor: 'Whatever course we may hereafter take must rest solely on military considerations, and hence in the first instance regard to the safety of our detached garrisons in Afghanistan; to the security of our troops now in the field from unnecessary risks; and finally, to the re-establishment of our military reputation by the infliction upon the Afghans of some signal and decisive blow.' Those were brave words, if only they had been adhered to. But six weeks later his lordship was ordering Nott to evacuate Candahar and fall back on Quetta, until the season should permit further retirement to the Indus; and instructing Pollock, through the Commander-in-Chief, to withdraw without delay every British soldier from Jellalabad to Peshawur, except under certain specified eventualities, none of which were in course of occurrence. Pollock temporised, holding on to his advanced position by the plea of inability to retire for want of transport, claiming mildly to find discretionary powers in the Government instructions, and cautiously arguing in favour of an advance by a few marches to a region where better climate was to be found, and whence he might bring to bear stronger pressure for the liberation of the prisoners. Nott was a narrower man than Pollock. When he got his orders he regarded them as strictly binding, no matter how unpalatable the injunctions. 'I shall not lose a moment,' he wrote, 'in making arrangements to carry out my orders, without turning to the right or the left, and without inquiring into the reasons for the measures enjoined, whatever our own opinions or wishes may be.' He reluctantly began preparations for withdrawal. Carriage was ordered up from Quetta, and a brigade was despatched to withdraw the garrison of Khelat-i-Ghilzai, and to destroy the fort which Craigie had so long and valiantly defended.

It would be tedious to detail the vacillations, the obscurities, and the tortuosities of Lord Ellenborough's successive communications to his two Generals in Afghanistan. Pollock had been permitted to remain about Jellalabad until the autumn should bring cooler marching weather. Nott had been detained at Candahar by the necessity for crushing menacing bodies of tribal levies, but as July waned his preparations for withdrawal were all but complete. On the 4th of that month Lord Ellenborough wrote to him, re-iterating injunctions for his withdrawal from Afghanistan, but permitting him the alternatives of retiring by the direct route along his line of communications over Quetta and Sukkur, or of boxing the compass by the curiously circuitous 'retirement' via Ghuznee, Cabul, and Jellalabad. Pollock, for his part, was permitted, if he thought proper, to advance on Cabul in order to facilitate Nott's withdrawal, if the latter should elect to 'retreat' by the circuitous route which has just been described.

One does not care to characterise the 'heads I win, tails you lose' policy of a Governor-General who thus shuffled off his responsibility upon two soldiers who previously had been sedulously restricted within narrow if varying limits. Their relief from those trammels set them free, and it was their joy to accept the devolved responsibility, and to act with soldierly initiative and vigour. The chief credit

of the qualified yet substantial triumph over official hesi-
tation certainly belongs to Pollock, who gently yet firmly
forced the hand of the Governor-General, while Nott's
merit was limited to a ready acceptance of the responsibility of a proffered option. A letter from Nott intimating
his determination to retire by way of Cabul and Jellalabad reached Pollock in the middle of August, who immediately advanced from Jellalabad; and his troops having
concentrated at Gundamuk, he marched from that position on 7th September, his second division, commanded
by M'Caskill, following next day. Pollock was woefully
short of transport, and therefore was compelled to leave
some troops behind at Gundamuk, and even then could
carry only half the complement of tentage. But his soldiers, who carried in their haversacks seven days' provisions, would gladly have marched without any baggage
at all, and the chief himself was eager to hurry forward,
for Nott had written that he expected to reach Cabul on
15th September, and Pollock was burning to be there first.
In the Jugdulluk Pass, on the 8th, he found the Ghilzais in
considerable force on the heights. Regardless of a heavy
artillery fire they stood their ground, and so galled Pollock's troops with sharp discharges from their jezails that
it became necessary to send infantry against them. They
were dislodged from the mountain they had occupied
by a portion of the Jellalabad brigade, led by gallant old
General Sale, who had his usual luck in the shape of a
wound.

This Jugdulluk fighting was, however, little more than
a skirmish, and Pollock's people were to experience more
severe opposition before they should emerge from the
passes on to the Cabul plain. On the morning of the 13th
the concentrated force had quitted its camp in the Tezeen
valley, and had committed itself without due precaution

to the passage of the ravine beyond, when the Afghan levies with which Akbar Khan had manned the flanking heights, opened their fire. The Sirdar had been dissuaded by Captain Troup, one of his prisoners, from attempting futile negotiations, and advised not to squander lives in useless opposition. Akbar had replied that he was too deeply committed to recede, and that his people were bent on fighting. They were not baulked in the aspiration, which assuredly their opponents shared with at least equal zeal. Pollock's advance-guard was about the middle of the defile, when the enemy were suddenly discovered blocking the pass in front, and holding the heights which Pollock's light troops should have crowned in advance of the column. Akbar's force was calculated to be about 15,000 strong, and the Afghans fought resolutely against the British regiments which forced their way up the heights on the right and left. The ghazees dashed down to meet the red soldiers halfway, and up among the precipices there were many hand-to-hand encounters, in which the sword and the bayonet fought out the issue. The Afghans made their last stand on the rocky summit of the Huft Kotul; but from this commanding position they were finally driven by Broadfoot's bloodthirsty little Goorkhas, who, hillmen themselves from their birth, chased the Afghans from crag to crag, using their fell kookeries as they pursued. It was Akbar Khan's last effort, and the quelling of it cost Pollock the trivial loss of thirty-two killed and 130 wounded. There was no more opposition, and it was well for the Afghans, for the awful spectacles presented in the Khoord Cabul Pass traversed on the following day, kindled in Pollock's soldiers a white heat of fury. 'The bodies,' wrote Backhouse in his unpublished diary, 'lay in heaps of fifties and hundreds, our gun wheels crushing the bones of our late comrades at every yard for four or five miles;

indeed, the whole march from Gundamuk to Cabul may be said to have been over the bodies of the massacred army.' Pollock marched unmolested to Cabul on the 15th, and camped on the old racecourse to the east of the city.

Nott, in evacuating Candahar, divided his force into two portions, the weaker of which General England took back to India by Quetta and Sukkur, while on August 9th Nott himself, with two European battalions, the 'beautiful sepoy regiments' of which he had a right to be proud, and his field guns, marched away from Candahar, his face set towards Cabul. His march was uneventful until about midway between Khelat-i-Ghilzai and Ghuznee, when on the 28th the cavalry, unsupported and badly handled in a stupid and unauthorised foray, lost severely in officers and men, took to flight in panic, and so gave no little encouragement to the enemy hanging on Nott's flank. Two days later Shumshoodeen, the Afghan leader, drew up some 10,000 men in order of battle on high ground left of the British camp. Nott attacked with vigour, advancing to turn the Afghan left. In reprisal the enemy threw their strength on his left, supporting their jezail fire with artillery, whereupon Nott changed front to the left, deployed, and then charged. The Afghans did not wait for close quarters, and Nott was no more seriously molested. Reaching the vicinity of Ghuznee on September 5th, he cleared away the hordes hanging on the heights which encircle the place. During the night the Afghans evacuated Ghuznee. Soon after daylight the British flag was waving from the citadel. Having fulfilled Lord Ellenborough's ridiculous order to carry away from the tomb of Sultan Mahmoud in the environs of Ghuznee, the supposititious gates of Somnath, a once famous Hindoo shrine in the Bombay province of Kattiawar, Nott marched onward unmolested till within a couple of marches of Cabul, when near Maidan he had some stubborn fighting with an Afghan force which tried ineffectually to block his way. On the 17th he marched into camp four miles west of Cabul, whence he could discern, not with entire complacency, the British ensign already flying from the Balla Hissar, for Pollock had won the race to Cabul by a couple of days.

For months there had been negotiations for the release of the British prisoners whom Akbar Khan had kept in durance ever since they came into his hands in the course of the disastrous retreat from Cabul in January, but they had been unsuccessful, and now it was known that the unfortunate company of officers, women, and children, had been carried off westward into the hill country of Bamian. Nott's officers, as the Candahar column was nearing Cabul, had more than once urged him to detach a brigade in the direction of Bamian in the hope of effecting a rescue of the prisoners, but he had steadily refused, leaning obstinately on the absence from the instructions sent him by Government of any permission to engage in the enterprise of attempting their release. He was not less brusque in the intimation of his declinature when Pollock gave him the opportunity to send a force in support of Sir Richmond Shakespear, whom, with a detachment of Kuzzilbash horse, Pollock had already despatched on the mission of attempting the liberation of the prisoners. The narrow old soldier argued doggedly that Government 'had thrown the prisoners overboard.' Why, then, should he concern himself with their rescue? If his superior officer should give him a firm order, of course he would obey, but he would obey under protest. Pollock disdained to impose so enviable a duty on a recalcitrant man, and committed to Sale the honourable and welcome service—all the more welcome to that officer because his wife and daughter were among the captives. At the head of his Jellalabad brigade, he was to push forward by forced marches on the track of Shakespear and his horsemen.

The strange and bitter experiences of the captives, from that miserable January Sabbath day on which they passed under the 'protection' of Akbar Khan until the mid-September noon when Shakespear galloped into their midst, are recorded in full and interesting detail in Lady Sale's journal, in Vincent Eyre's Captivity , and in Colin Mackenzie's biography published under the title of Storms and Sunshine of a Soldier's Life . Here it is possible only briefly to summarise the chief incidents of the captivity. The unanimous testimony of the released prisoners was to the effect that Akbar Khan, violent, bloody, and passionate man though he was, behaved toward them with kindness and a certain rude chivalry. They remained for nearly three months at Budiabad, living in great squalor and discomfort. For the whole party there were but five rooms, each of which was occupied by from five to ten officers and ladies, the few soldiers and non-commissioned officers, who were mostly wounded, being quartered in sheds and cellars. Mackenzie drily remarks that the hardships of the common lot, and the close intimacy of prison life, brought into full relief good and evil qualities; 'conventional polish was a good deal rubbed off and replaced by a plainness of speech quite unheard of in good society.' Ladies and gentlemen were necessitated to occupy the same room during the night, but the men 'cleared out' early in the morning, leaving the ladies to themselves. The dirt and vermin of their habitation were abominably offensive to people to whom scrupulous cleanliness was a second nature. But the captives were allowed to take exercise within a limited range; they had among them a few books, and an old newspaper occasionally came on to them from Jellalabad, with which place a fitful correspondence in cypher was surreptitiously maintained. They had a few packs of playing cards; they made for themselves backgammon and draught-boards, and when in good spirits they sometimes played hopscotch and blindman's-buff with the children of the party. The Sundays were always kept scrupulously, Lawrence and Mackenzie conducting the service in turn.

The earthquake which shook down the fortifications of Jellalabad brought their rickety fort about the ears of the captives. Several escaped narrowly with their lives when walls and roofs yawned and crumbled, and all had to turn out and sleep in the courtyard, where they suffered from cold and saturating dews. After the defeat of Akbar by the Jellalabad garrison on April 7th, there was keen expectation that Sale would march to their rescue, but he came not, and there were rumours among the guards of their impending massacre in revenge for the crushing reverse Akbar had experienced. Presently, however, Mahomed Shah Khan, Akbar's lieutenant, arrived full of courtesy and reassurance, but with the unwelcome intimation that the prisoners must prepare themselves to leave Budiabad at once, and move to a greater distance from Jellalabad and their friends. For some preparation was not a difficult task. 'All my worldly goods,' wrote Captain Johnson, 'might be stowed away in a towel.' Others who possessed heavier impedimenta, were lightened of the encumbrance by the Ghilzai Sirdar, who plundered indiscriminately. The European soldiers were left behind at Budiabad, and the band of ladies and gentlemen started on the afternoon of April 10th, in utter ignorance of their destination, under the escort of a strong band of Afghans. At the ford across the Cabul river the cavalcade found Akbar Khan wounded, haggard, and dejected, seated in a palanquin, which, weak as he was, he gave up to Ladies Macnaghten and Sale, who were ill. A couple of days were spent at Tezeen among the melancholy relics of the January slaughter, whence most of the party were carried several miles further into the southern mountains to the village of Zandeh, while General Elphinstone, whose end was fast approaching, remained in the Tezeen valley with Pottinger, Mackenzie, Eyre, and one or two others. On the evening of April 23d the poor General was finally released from suffering of mind and body. Akbar, who when too late had offered to free him, sent the body down to Jellalabad under a guard, and accompanied by Moore the General's soldier servant; and Elphinstone lies with Colonel Dennie and the dead of the defence of Jellalabad in their nameless graves in a waste place within the walls of that place. Toward the end of May the captives were moved up the passes to the vicinity of Cabul, where Akbar Khan was now gradually attaining the ascendant. Prince Futteh Jung, however, still held out in the Balla Hissar, and intermittent firing was heard as the weary cortège of prisoners reached a fort about three miles short of Cabul, which the ladies of the proprietor's zenana had evacuated in their favour. Here they lived if not in contentment at least in considerable comfort and amenity. They had the privacy of a delightful garden, and enjoyed the freedom of bathing in the adjacent river. After the strife between Akbar Khan and Futteh Jung ceased they were even permitted to exchange visits with their countrymen, the hostages quartered on the Balla Hissar. They were able to obtain money from the Cabul usurers, and thus to supply themselves with suitable clothing and additions to their rations, and their mails from India and Jellalabad were forwarded to them without hindrance. The summer months were passed in captivity, but it was no longer for them a captivity of squalor and wretchedness. Life was a good deal better worth living in the pleasant garden house on the bank of the Logur than it had been in the noisome squalor of Budiabad and the vermin-infested huddlement of Zandeh. But they still-lived under the long strain of anxiety and apprehension, for none of them knew what the morrow might bring forth. While residing in the pleasant quarters in the Logur valley the captives of the passes were joined by nine officers, who were the captives of Ghuznee. After the capitulation the latter had been treated with cruel harshness, shut up in one small room, and debarred from fresh air and exercise. Colonel Palmer, indeed, had undergone the barbarity of torture in the endeavour to force him to disclose the whereabouts of treasure which he was suspected of having buried.

Akbar had full and timely intimation of the mutual intention of the British generals at Jellalabad and Candahar to march on Cabul, and did not fail to recognise of what value to him in extremity might be his continued possession of the prisoners. They had been warned of their probable deportation to the remote and rugged Bamian; and the toilsome journey thither was begun on the evening of August 25th. A couple of ailing families alone, with a surgeon in charge of them, were allowed to remain behind; all the others, hale and sick, had to travel, the former on horseback, the latter carried in camel panniers. The escort consisted of an irregular regiment of Afghan infantry commanded by one Saleh Mahomed Khan, who when a subadar serving in one of the Shah's Afghan regiments had deserted to Dost Mahomed. The wayfarers, female as well as male, wore the Afghan costume, in order that they might attract as little notice as possible.

Bamian was reached on September 3d, where the wretchedness of the quarters contrasted vividly with the amenity of those left behind on the Cabul plain. But the wretchedness of Bamian was not to be long endured. An intimacy had been struck up between Captain Johnson and Saleh Mahomed, and the latter cautiously hinted that a reward and a pension might induce him to carry his charges into the British camp. On September 11th there was a private meeting between the Afghan commandant and three British officers, Pottinger, Johnson, and Lawrence. Saleh Mahomed intimated the receipt of instructions from the Sirdar to carry the prisoners over the Hindoo Koosh into Khooloom, and leave them there to seeming hopeless captivity. But on the other hand a messenger had reached Saleh from Mohun Lal with the assurance that General Pollock, if he restored the prisoners, would ensure him a reward of 20,000 rupees, and a life pension of 12,000 rupees a year. Saleh Mahomed demanded and received a guarantee from the British officers; and the captives bound themselves to make good from their own resources their redemption money. The Afghan ex-Subadar proved himself honest; the captives were captives no longer, and they proceeded to assert themselves in the masterful British manner. They hoisted the national flag; Pottinger became once again the high-handed 'political,' and ordered the local chiefs to come to his durbar and receive dresses of honour. Their fort was put into a state of defence, and a store of provisions was gathered in case of a siege. But in mid-September came the tidings that Akbar had been defeated at Tezeen, and had fled no one knew whither, whereupon the self-emancipated party set out on the march to Cabul. At noon of the 17th they passed into the safe guardianship of Shakespear and his horsemen. Three days later, within a march of Cabul, there was reached the column which Sale had taken out, and on September 21st Pollock greeted the company of men and women whose rescue had been wrought out by his cool, strong steadfastness.

Little more remains to be told. There was an Afghan force still in arms at Istalif, a beautiful village of the inveterately hostile Kohistanees; a division marched to attack it, carried the place by assault, burnt part of it, and severely smote the garrison. Utter destruction was the fate of Charikar, the capital of the Kohistan, where Codrington's Goorkha regiment had been destroyed. Pollock determined to 'set a mark' on Cabul to commemorate the retribution which the British had exacted. He spared the Balla Hissar, and abstained from laying the city in ruins, contenting himself with the destruction of the principal bazaar, through which the heads of Macnaghten and Burnes had been paraded, and in which their mangled bodies had been exposed. Prince Futteh Jung, tired of his vicissitudes in the character of an Afghan monarch, ceded what of a throne he possessed to another puppet of his race, and gladly accompanied the British armies to India. Other waifs of the wreck of a nefarious and disastrous enterprise, among them old Zemaun Khan, who had been our friend throughout, and the family of the ill-fated Shah Soojah, were well content to return to the exile which afforded safety and quietude. There also accompanied the march of the humane Pollock a great number of the mutilated and crippled camp followers of Elphinstone's army who had escaped with their lives from its destruction. On the 12th of October the forces of Pollock and of Nott turned their backs on Cabul, which no British army was again to see for nearly forty years, and set out on their march down the passes. Jellalabad and Ali Musjid were partially destroyed in passing. Pollock's division reached Peshawur without loss, thanks to the precautions of its chief; but with M'Caskill and Nott the indomitable Afghans had the last word, cutting off their stragglers, capturing their baggage, and in the final skirmish killing and wounding some sixty men of Nott's command.

Of the bombastic and grotesque paeans of triumph emitted by Lord Ellenborough, whose head had been turned by a success to which he had but scantly contributed, nothing need now be said, nor of the garish pageant with which he received the armies as they re-entered British territory at Ferozepore. As they passed down through the Punjaub, Dost Mahomed passed up on his way to reoccupy the position from which he had been driven. And so ended the first Afghan war, a period of history in which no redeeming features are perceptible except the defence of Jellalabad, the dogged firmness of Nott, and Pollock's noble and successful constancy of purpose. Beyond this effulgence there spreads a sombre welter of misrepresentation and unscrupulousness, intrigue, moral deterioration, and dishonour unspeakable.

LEONAUR

ALSO FROM LEONAUR

AVAILABLE IN SOFTCOVER OR HARDCOVER WITH DUST JACKET

SEPOYS, SIEGE & STORM *by Charles John Griffiths*—The Experiences of a young officer of H.M.'s 61st Regiment at Ferozepore, Delhi ridge and at the fall of Delhi during the Indian mutiny 1857.

CAMPAIGNING IN ZULULAND *by W. E. Montague*—Experiences on campaign during the Zulu war of 1879 with the 94th Regiment.

THE STORY OF THE GUIDES *by G. J. Younghusband*—The Exploits of the Soldiers of the famous Indian Army Regiment from the northwest frontier 1847 - 1900..

ZULU: 1879 *by D.C.F. Moodie & the Leonaur Editors*—The Anglo-Zulu War of 1879 from contemporary sources: First Hand Accounts, Interviews, Dispatches, Official Documents & Newspaper Reports.

THE RECOLLECTIONS OF SKINNER OF SKINNER'S HORSE *by James Skinner*—James Skinner and his 'Yellow Boys' Irregular cavalry in the wars of India between the British, Mahratta, Rajput, Mogul, Sikh & Pindarree Forces.

TOMMY ATKINS' WAR STORIES 14 FIRST HAND ACCOUNTS—Fourteen first hand accounts from the ranks of the British Army during Queen Victoria's Empire Original & True Battle Stories Recollections of the Indian Mutiny With the 49th in the Crimea With the Guards in Egypt The Charge of the Six Hundred With Wolseley in Ashanti Alma, Inkermann and Magdala With the Gunners at Tel-el-Kebir Russian Guns and Indian Rebels Rough Work in the Crimea In the Maori Rising Facing the Zulus From Sebastopol to Lucknow Sent to Save Gordon On the March to Chitral Tommy by Rudyard Kipling

CHASSEUR OF 1914 *by Marcel Dupont*—Experiences of the twilight of the French Light Cavalry by a young officer during the early battles of the great war in Europe.

TROOP HORSE & TRENCH *by R. A. Lloyd*—The experiences of a British Lifeguardsman of the household cavalry fighting on the western front during the First World War 1914-18.

THE EAST AFRICAN MOUNTED RIFLES *by C. J. Wilson*—Experiences of the campaign in the East African bush during the First World War.

THE FIGHTING CAMELIERS *by Frank Reid*—The exploits of the Imperial Camel Corps in the desert and Palestine campaigns of the First World War.

LEONAUR

ALSO FROM LEONAUR

AVAILABLE IN SOFTCOVER OR HARDCOVER WITH DUST JACKET

THE COMPLEAT RIFLEMAN HARRIS *by Benjamin Harris as told to & transcribed by Captain Henry Curling*—The adventures of a soldier of the 95th (Rifles) during the Peninsular Campaign of the Napoleonic Wars

WITH WELLINGTON'S LIGHT CAVALRY *by William Tomkinson*—The Experiences of an officer of the 16th Light Dragoons in the Peninsular and Waterloo campaigns of the Napoleonic Wars.

SERGEANT BOURGOGNE *by Adrien Bourgogne*—With Napoleon's Imperial Guard in the Russian Campaign and on the Retreat from Moscow 1812 - 13.

SWORDS OF HONOUR *by Henry Newbolt & Stanley L. Wood*—The Careers of Six Outstanding Officers from the Napoleonic Wars, the Wars for India and the American Civil War, with dozens of illustrations by Stanley L. Wood.

SURTEES OF THE RIFLES *by William Surtees*—A Soldier of the 95th (Rifles) in the Peninsular campaign of the Napoleonic Wars.

ENSIGN BELL IN THE PENINSULAR WAR *by George Bell*—The Experiences of a young British Soldier of the 34th Regiment 'The Cumberland Gentlemen' in the Napoleonic wars.

HUSSAR IN WINTER *by Alexander Gordon*—A British Cavalry Officer during the retreat to Corunna in the Peninsular campaign of the Napoleonic Wars.

NAPOLEONIC WAR STORIES *by Sir Arthur Quiller-Couch*—Tales of soldiers, spies, battles & sieges from the Peninsular & Waterloo campaigns.

JOURNALS OF ROBERT ROGERS OF THE RANGERS *by Robert Rogers*—The exploits of Rogers & the Rangers in his own words during 1755-1761 in the French & Indian War.

KERSHAW'S BRIGADE VOLUME 1 *by D. Augustus Dickert*—Manassas, Seven Pines, Sharpsburg (Antietam), Fredricksburg, Chancellorsville, Gettysburg, Chickamauga, Chattanooga, Fort Sanders & Bean Station..

KERSHAW'S BRIGADE VOLUME 2 *by D. Augustus Dickert*—At the wilderness, Cold Harbour, Petersburg, The Shenandoah Valley and Cedar Creek.

A TIGER ON HORSEBACK *by L. March Phillips*—The Experiences of a Trooper & Officer of Rimington's Guides - The Tigers - during the Anglo-Boer war 1899 - 1902.

LEONAUR

ALSO FROM LEONAUR

AVAILABLE IN SOFTCOVER OR HARDCOVER WITH DUST JACKET

CAPTAIN OF THE 95th (Rifles) *by Jonathan Leach*—An officer of Wellington's Sharpshooters during the Peninsular, South of France and Waterloo Campaigns of the Napoleonic Wars.

THE KHAKEE RESSALAH *by Robert Henry Wallace Dunlop*—Service & adventure with the Meerut volunteer horse during the Indian mutiny 1857-1858

BUGLER AND OFFICER OF THE RIFLES *by William Green & Harry Smith* With the 95th (Rifles) during the Peninsular & Waterloo Campaigns of the Napoleonic Wars

BAYONETS, BUGLES AND BONNETS *by James 'Thomas' Todd*—Experiences of hard soldiering with the 71st Foot - the Highland Light Infantry - through many battles of the Napoleonic wars including the Peninsular & Waterloo Campaigns

A NORFOLK SOLDIER IN THE FIRST SIKH WAR *by J W Baldwin*—Experiences of a private of H.M. 9th Regiment of Foot in the battles for the Punjab, India 1845-46

A CAVALRY OFFICER DURING THE SEPOY REVOLT *by A.R.D. Mackenzie*—Experiences with the 3rd Bengal Light Cavalry, the Guides and Sikh Irregular Cavalry from the outbreak to Delhi and Lucknow

THE ADVENTURES OF A LIGHT DRAGOON *by George Farmer & G.R. Gleig*—A cavalryman during the Peninsular & Waterloo Campaigns, in captivity & at the siege of Bhurtpore, India

THE COMPLEAT RIFLEMAN HARRIS *by Benjamin Harris as told to & transcribed by Captain Henry Curling*—The adventures of a soldier of the 95th (Rifles) during the Peninsular Campaign of the Napoleonic Wars

THE RED DRAGOON *by W.J. Adams*—With the 7th Dragoon Guards in the Cape of Good Hope against the Boers & the Kaffir tribes during the 'war of the axe' 1843-48

THE LIFE OF THE REAL BRIGADIER GERARD - Volume 1 - THE YOUNG HUSSAR 1782 - 1807 *by Jean-Baptiste De Marbot*—A French Cavalryman Of the Napoleonic Wars at Marengo, Austerlitz, Jena, Eylau & Friedland

THE LIFE OF THE REAL BRIGADIER GERARD Volume 2 IMPERIAL AIDE-DE-CAMP 1807 - 1811 *by Jean-Baptiste De Marbot*—A French Cavalryman of the Napoleonic Wars at Saragossa, Landshut, Eckmuhl, Ratisbon, Aspern-Essling, Wagram, Busaco & Torres Vedras

LEONAUR

ALSO FROM LEONAUR
AVAILABLE IN SOFTCOVER OR HARDCOVER WITH DUST JACKET

EW2 EYEWITNESS TO WAR SERIES
CAPTAIN OF THE 95th (Rifles) *by Jonathan Leach*

An officer of Wellington's Sharpshooters during the
Peninsular, South of France and Waterloo Campaigns
of the Napoleonic Wars.

SOFTCOVER   : **ISBN 1-84677-001-7**
HARDCOVER : **ISBN 1-84677-016-5**

WFI THE WARFARE FICTION SERIES
NAPOLEONIC WAR STORIES
by Sir Arthur Quiller-Couch

Tales of soldiers, spies, battles & Sieges from the
Peninsular & Waterloo campaigns

SOFTCOVER   : **ISBN 1-84677-003-3**
HARDCOVER : **ISBN 1-84677-014-9**

EWI EYEWITNESS TO WAR SERIES
RIFLEMAN COSTELLO *by Edward Costello*

The adventures of a soldier of the 95th (Rifles) in the
Peninsular & Waterloo Campaigns of the Napoleonic wars.

SOFTCOVER   : **ISBN 1-84677-000-9**
HARDCOVER : **ISBN 1-84677-018-1**

MCI THE MILITARY COMMANDERS SERIES
JOURNALS OF ROBERT ROGERS OF THE RANGERS *by Robert Rogers*

The exploits of Rogers & the Rangers in his own words
during 1755-1761 in the French & Indian War.

SOFTCOVER   : **ISBN 1-84677-002-5**
HARDCOVER : **ISBN 1-84677-010-6**

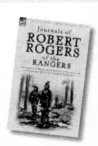

Lightning Source UK Ltd.
Milton Keynes UK
09 December 2009
147255UK00001B/173/A